LIFE IS IMPOSSIBLE
AND THAT'S GOOD NEWS

"Nick Lannon has combined humor, delightful but gut-grabbing illustrations from life, and the heart of a pastoral 'man for others', to create a kind of masterpiece, a surprising classic. I say that aware of what I am saying. *Life Is Impossib!   d That's Good News* is a short, accessible cl~~~~

How'd he do it?, yo'   t Nick has accessed the Well o  life in such a way that you rea·   ·ling. Impromptu. And not in   ., when we rise' (Donovan, 1965)."

- Paul F. M. Zahl
Author of *Grace in Practice: A Theology of Everyday Life*

"Whoever told us that the experience of Christian living was one of escalating progress lied to us. It is, rather, a glorious impossibility. And while that may seem to be a depressing sentiment, it is actually liberating to the core. Because it is only as we come to terms with our weakness and ongoing failure that we come to know God's strength and ongoing success on our behalf.

My good friend Nick Lannon has written a real, earthy, honest book that will set you free to admit that you can't do it. But he doesn't leave you there. He points beautifully and creatively to the One who did it for you. Thank you, Nick, for reminding me that IT IS FINISHED. I keep forgetting."

- Tullian Tchividjian
Author of *One Way Love: Inexhaustible Grace for an Exhausted World*

"Nick Lannon unveils to us the beauty of grace hidden in the impossibilities of life. Masterfully clear and imminently practical, this book puts flesh on theology, roots it in daily life, and demonstrates over and over that when we run into the brick wall of the impossible, we are actually at the very door that opens to Christ's saving work."

- Chad Bird

Author of *Night Driving* and *Your God Is Too Glorious*

"To read this book is to receive a diagnosis: Life is not just hard; we are weary and heavy-laden because life is impossible. But to read this book is also to hear a word that delivers: There is one who lived, died, and lives again and who, through the miracle of mercy, takes the weight of our lives off of our shoulders and carries it himself as he says, 'Come unto me, I will give you rest.' *Life Is Impossible* is more than words on the page; it is a proclamation of the word that shows us we need a saviour and the proclamation of the word that, like the finger of John the Baptist, points away from our life as it points to the lamb, the saviour who takes away the sins of the world."

- Dr. Jonathan A. Linebaugh

Editor of *God's Two Words: Law and Gospel in Lutheran and Reformed Traditions*

"Who in the world would want the opposite of 'your best life now'? Well, as it turns out, after encountering this book, I do. And I bet you will, too. Good news, told and illustrated well, tends to have that oddly freeing effect."

- Zac Hicks

Author of *The Worship Pastor*

LIFE IS IMPOSSIBLE

AND THAT'S GOOD NEWS

LIFE IS IMPOSSIBLE

AND THAT'S GOOD NEWS

BY NICK LANNON

*(husband of Ayola Lannon,
who is granddaughter of
Aunt Hazel Selvis!)*

A MOCKINGBIRD PUBLICATION

For Aya

And Hazel, Patrick, and Charlie

And in memory of Susan, who taught me to write

ACKNOWLEDGEMENTS

Thank you to Jady Koch, Jono Linebaugh, Tullian Tchividjian, and Paul Zahl. These four men taught me the Good News and gave me the words to express it. They are friends, pastors, and mentors to me. They know that they are sheep of Christ's own fold, lambs of his own flock, and sinners of his own redeeming. This book couldn't exist without them.

CONTENTS

INTRODUCTION ✓ 3|22|20

ALL IS LOST...
AND ALL IS NOT LOST

Robert Redford is lost at sea. He's about to die. I know, right? Not Robert Redford! Not the Sundance Kid! This paragon of strength and virility—I mean, look at those manly lines on his face—is the last person on earth we'd expect to find in this predicament. No one was better prepared for the voyage than he was...and yet he finds himself on the point of death. He's curled up, crying and alone, like an infant back in the womb. He's finally realized that the obstacles he's facing are impossible to overcome.

I have bad news. Actually, it's news that you probably already know...although you probably don't know that you know it. Here it is: you're just like Robert Redford. Your life is impossible. You can't do anything you want to do or be anything you want to be. I know, I know...my mother was wrong, too. Olympic athletes and celebrities who tell us that we can do anything we set our minds to? Also wrong. But you knew this, even if only subconsciously. Ask all the people who didn't win Olympic medals and who didn't "make it" in Hollywood. They know it, too. And those are just things that are obviously impossible. Things that seem simple turn out to be beyond our reach, too. Try deciding to not be in a bad mood. Or to stop a case of the giggles. Life is impossible. That's bad news.

But I have good news, too, and this you might not know: the fact that your life is impossible is actually *good* news. It's good news because of the Good News (capital "G," capital "N") about Jesus. That's what this book is about: the bad news that life is impossible, and the Good News that Jesus is the savior for those burdened with an impossible life.

There's no better way to introduce a book about the impossibility of life—and why it's good news—than the scene I described at the beginning of this introduction, the psychological climax of the nearly dialogue-free Robert Redford film *All Is Lost* (written and directed by J. C. Chandor). Redford stars as "Our Man," an aging-but-capable mariner who finds himself lost at sea. Apart from a bit of opening narration and a screamed expletive when he realizes that all might indeed be lost, the only dialogue in the film is Redford calling out to a couple of passing ships for help.

The ships don't stop. All is lost. *All Is Lost* is a film about ultimate powerlessness. More precisely, it's a film about the powerlessness of human beings to deal with what life can (and usually does) throw at them. It's about the impossible. At first blush, though, "our man" is anything but powerless. We first meet him as he wakes up to his sailboat filling with water. We watch as he assesses the damage and goes about fixing it, all with incredible calm and skill. I found myself thinking, within moments of the beginning of the film, "Well, I'd be dead already." But not our man. And that's the point.

All Is Lost is the story of an *Übermensch,* an almost superheroic Redford ready for anything…except the ultimate thing.

The ultimate thing in any sailing movie is, of course, a storm. But not just any storm. A storm that reduces our man to nothing. In a storm powerful enough, all the preparation, all the skill, and all the calm in the face of adversity just isn't enough. Our man is as ready to face this storm as a man in a sailboat (albeit with a broken radio) could possibly be. He's infinitely more ready than you or I would be. But it's not enough.

It's not too on-the-nose at this point to say that the viewer is meant to consider the situations in their lives in which their preparation isn't enough. Chandor has said explicitly in interviews that his intention was to bring moviegoers to a place in which they were forced to come to grips with their own mortality. This is a story meant to force you to confront the impossibility of your life, the incontrovertible fact that, no matter how ready you are, there will be situations that you cannot control, things that get the best of you.

It is a natural human impulse, I think, famously capitalized upon by the Boy Scouts, to assume that preparedness can solve any problem. If you go into the woods with the right maps, enough food and water, and appropriate bug repellant, you should be fine. Analogously, if you go out into the world with the right grounding in philosophy, having read the classics, and with an appropriately dry sense of humor, you should be fine. Until the storm comes. It's in the midst of the wind and waves that you realize your preparedness is insufficient. No one has put this feeling more succinctly than boxer Mike Tyson, who famously said that "everybody has a plan 'til they get punched in the mouth." I'm writing this book for people like me, who thought they were prepared, but who then got punched in the mouth.

Christians ought to understand this storm best, because we know where it comes from. It should be no surprise to see it brewing on the horizon; we've been trying to protect ourselves from it since Adam and Eve sewed fig leaves together in the Garden of Eden (Adam said, "'I heard the sound of you in the garden, and I was afraid...'" (Genesis 3:10, ESV*)). But what Christians all too often think is that they *can* be prepared enough—usually through things like spiritual disciplines and morally upright living—to survive the storm. They know the storm is going to be heavy—after all, there is no storm more powerful than God's judgment of and wrath toward sin—but they think that they can ride it out, perhaps with a little well-timed help from Jesus. They're wrong. That's what this book is about. The storm is too vicious. Nothing can be done to escape it. In the face of the killer storm of the almighty power of God...all is lost. This is the story of the counter-intuitive freedom that comes from the realization that the problems you face aren't difficult ones but impossible ones.

At the key moment in *All Is Lost*, our man is reduced to something like infancy, unable to affect his fate at all. He's in a life raft, in the midst of the storm, in the fetal position. He has his hands over his ears and his eyes squeezed shut, like a child being told something he doesn't want to hear. The announcement he's hearing is God's first word out of the storm: you're going to die. Our man can no longer think of life's problems as difficult. The truth is literally drowning him: his life is impossible. That seems like terrible news. All is lost. And yet, all is not lost.

"You're going to die" may be God's first word out of the storm, but it's not God's final word. The other thing that Christians know about the storm is that it ends. After all, Jesus announced that "it is finished" as he hung on the cross, guaranteeing victory to all who trust in him for salvation from the storm.

Our man's rescue (in the film) is a miracle. It can be described in no other way. He drifts by accident into an active

---

*All Scripture references are ESV, unless otherwise noted.

shipping lane but is unable to flag down either of two tankers, one of which passes so close to him that I thought he might just grab hold as it went by. Finally, he drifts out of the other side of the shipping lane. Grasping at straws, he burns his life raft in an effort to alert a third ship, but that doesn't seem to be working either. The ship isn't stopping. As he floats beside the burning raft, he even literally stops treading water, deciding to drown. He gives up. All is lost. Then, everything changes.

It is only when all of our self-salvation efforts are exhausted, it is only when we decide to stop treading water that we will call out for a savior who exists outside of us. That call is answered by God's second and final word out of the storm: a calm sea, and a savior walking across the water.

First, all is lost. Then, all is not lost. Then, salvation. Then, the shadow of a boat. Then, a hand reaching down beneath the surface of the water. Our man is rescued, and so are we. When all is lost to us, almighty God proves that all is not lost to him.

This world—the one you see if you look up from behind the pages of this book—will tell you again and again that life is difficult. Too often, the church will join that chorus, claiming that the life of the Christian is difficult, too. I've written this book for those who—like me—set out on the Christian journey like Robert Redford in *All Is Lost:* prepared for a difficult ride and convinced that Jesus would be there to help when things got overwhelming. But life isn't difficult. Following Christ's example isn't difficult. Both are impossible. Both will leave you—again, like Redford—curled up in the fetal position, calling out for help. That life is impossible is worse news than perhaps you were expecting…but it only throws the goodness of the Good News into sharper relief: God delights in accomplishing the impossible. The impossible work of God makes an impossible life good news: it means you don't have to save yourself. God has done that for you.

CHAPTER 1 ✓ 19/23

WE ALWAYS DO THE HARD THING

At the very beginning of the otherwise completely forgettable *Mission: Impossible 2*, Anthony Hopkins is giving Ethan Hunt, played by Tom Cruise, his mission. After Cruise complains that it sounds difficult, Hopkins has this great line: "Mr. Hunt, this isn't mission difficult, it's mission impossible. 'Difficult' should be a walk in the park for you." And, of course, as in all the *Mission: Impossible* films and TV shows, the mission *does* turn out to just be difficult—rather than impossible—because the IMF and Ethan Hunt always win the day.

And this is an interesting thing, isn't it? Even in a movie called *Mission: Impossible*, the mission *isn't* actually impossible. This is the lens through which we look at the world and our lives, this *Mission: Difficult* lens: that many things are difficult, but very few things are impossible. In point of fact, the exact opposite is actually true: almost everything in life that's worth anything is impossible.

We humans, though, tend to think that impossible is rare. We approach our life as though it's merely difficult. The many "oughts" of our lives are goals that we feel that we can and should accomplish. We should love our neighbor. Difficult, we think, but possible. We should honor our fathers and mothers.

Difficult, but possible. We should be patient with those people in our lives who get on our last nerves. Difficult, but possible. These difficult things can be the most mundane of goals, too: turning that frown upside down, for instance. Difficult, but possible. Not being so uptight. Difficult, but possible. Losing those pesky ten to fifteen pounds. Difficult, but possible. Until we try to do it. I mean, think about it. Reflect on the last time you were really angry. Could you have just decided not to be mad? Of course not. If you could have, wouldn't you have? In practice, as good as it sounds to simply decide not to be mad, it's impossible. Try *actually* loving your neighbor—not just pretending to—when they're being unlovable. Impossible. Try just deciding to relax when the situation is stressful. Impossible.

In the final season of the TV show *Frasier*, there's an episode called "Murder Most Maris" which wonderfully illustrates the impossibility of things that we normally think of as merely difficult. In the episode, Maris Crane, the ex-wife of Frasier's younger brother Niles, is accused of murder. Niles is implicated as a possible accessory for lending her an antique crossbow, which became the murder weapon. His life swirling out of control, Niles firmly "chooses" to be calm. Martin, the Crane boys' father, observes of his younger son, "Wow! He's really holding up well!" "A little too well," Frasier grumbles. "I'm starting to fear that he's not dealing with his emotions at all!" "Right," Martin says, "That's the whole secret to holding up!"

This exchange illustrates a disconnect that people, and especially Christians, experience. How important—if it's important at all—is the difference between what is on our outsides (what is visible to the world) and what is on our insides (what we keep to ourselves)? What is real? What is pretend? Which is more powerful? I think many people would agree with Martin, that hiding what's really going on is a skill. The grieving spouse who gets right back to dating, or the mourning parent who always has a smile on his face. Often, this kind of bearing up is referred to as strength. But what is the value of this kind of strength? Is it even possible to control ourselves in this way? Or can we only choose to pretend?

As "Murder Most Maris" continues, Niles' life becomes harder and harder to deal with, the problems keep mounting up, and we can tell that he's having more and more trouble "putting on a good face." Yet, all the while, he is doggedly insistent that everything is fine. Finally, he goes to Café Nervosa (the inevitable coffee shop where everyone is always hanging out), orders a coffee and asks for a straw, only to be told that the person ahead of him in line just got the last one. This proves to be the (hilariously literal) last straw, and Niles has a total nervous breakdown, stripping naked in the coffee shop and having to be removed by those who love him. His act is revealed to be a sham; "choosing to be calm" turned out to be impossible after all.[1]

The terrible result of going through our lives thinking that all the obstacles we face are merely difficult is that we try to handle them on our own. The more we commit ourselves to accomplishing the "difficult" things, the more we become Niles Crane: a ticking time bomb. You think your life is hard? I've got worse news than that. Your life is impossible.

A PRESIDENT AND A LEPER

In a 1962 speech at Rice University, President John F. Kennedy talked about his decision to move the American space program from low to high gear. He called it one of the most important decisions that he would make as president. You've probably heard the clip on TV or in a movie:

> But why, some say, the moon? Why choose this as
> our goal? And they may well ask, "Why climb the

highest mountain? Why, 35 years ago, fly the Atlantic? Why does Rice play Texas?" We choose to go to the moon in this decade and do the other things, not because they are easy, but because they are hard, because that goal will serve to organize and measure the best of our energies and skills, because that challenge is one that we are willing to accept, one we are unwilling to postpone, and one we intend to win.

Rousing, right? Makes you want to go out and run through a wall, or fight a giant or something! Or, you know, fly to the moon. The reason it's so rousing is that Kennedy is speaking to that latent Ethan Hunt in all of us. I want to do the hard things. I want to climb the highest mountain. I want to fly to the moon. I want to do something that'll make people stand up and cheer. Don't you? We want to do the hard things, and so we celebrate those who do. We laud athletic champions, but don't we celebrate the champion all the more if he or she can be said to have done it "by themselves"? The more difficult the feat, the better, and the more celebrated. When we want to make our mark, we search out a challenge, and we can get sort of angry when someone tries to make the challenge we've set for ourselves easier. We say things like, "You brought a portable GPS on our hike? But the risk of getting lost is the whole point!"

In 2 Kings 5, Naaman, an army commander, gets similarly angry when it turns out that he can easily have the thing that he thought he'd have to work hard to get. You see, Naaman, powerful in the army as he is, has a problem. He's got leprosy. But, luckily, his army has just recently captured a slave girl from Samaria, and she says she knows of a prophet who can heal him! So Naaman sets off on this long journey from Damascus to Samaria outfitted with ten talents of silver, six thousand shekels of gold, and ten sets of garments to purchase the healing. You should know that that's 750 pounds of silver and 150 pounds of gold. It's a royal amount of money. He gets to Samaria, and after meeting the king, Elisha the prophet hears of his condition. This is when the story gets interesting.

When Naaman arrives at Elisha's house with all of his horses and chariots, the prophet sends a messenger to him, saying, "Go and wash in the Jordan seven times, and your flesh shall be restored, and you shall be clean" (5:10). Naaman is furious: "I thought that he would surely come out to me and stand and call upon the name of the LORD his God, and wave his hand over the place and cure the leper. Are not Abana and Pharpar, the rivers of Damascus, better than all the waters of Israel? Could I not wash in them and be clean?" (5:11-12). So he starts to go off in a huff. The Bible says he went away in a rage. But his servants say, "Wait a minute! If the prophet had commanded you to do something hard, would you not have done it? So why aren't you going to do it when he only asked you to do something easy?" So Naaman finally acquiesces and does the easy thing—washing in the dirty Jordan River—and is made clean.

See, Naaman is like Kennedy. Kennedy said that we choose to do the hard thing because it "measures the best of our energies and skills." In other words, we do the hard thing because it will prove how awesome we are. We are addicted to seeming and feeling awesome. There's a wall of photos in my local YMCA of members who are in the Y's "Livestrong" program. Each comes with a quote from the member. Most of them say things like "Committed to doing my best" or "Taking it one day at a time," but one of them puts it just this bluntly: "I am addicted to feeling strong." Naaman is also addicted. He comes to Samaria intending to overwhelm the prophet with his riches. He's got all this silver and gold and beautiful clothing, and he rolls up to Elisha's house with all his horses and chariots. He wants Elisha to notice how awesome he is.

How demeaning then that Elisha doesn't even come out! He sends a servant out to tell Naaman to go wash in the Jordan seven times. It's sort of the "Thank you, come again" convenience-store-shopping-trip of healings: as little effort by the healer as possible. And Naaman is not happy. He's not happy because he's been embarrassed. Elisha seems to have implied that Naaman's not even worth getting up for, right? Naaman is somehow not worthy of Elisha's full attention, and there's no quicker way to make someone mad than to make them feel unworthy of you.

Naaman is angry for another—seemingly odd—reason, too: the solution he's given is so simple! "I thought that for me he would surely come out, and stand and call on the name of the Lord his God, and would wave his hand over the spot, and cure the leprosy!" When he's told to just go to the local river to wash, he thinks that that's something he could have just as well done for himself. He wants a complicated ritual, or a recipe with all sorts of steps that he has to follow. He's angry that he's not getting a long assignment. This seems incredibly counter-intuitive on the surface, but when you think about it, it makes perfect sense: if Naaman can't purchase this healing, he wants to earn it by showing Elisha that he's willing to do any arcane ritual that the prophet can come up with. Crazy, right? But this is a crazy that we all share.

Remember when your dad told you that you should do something or other because it would put hair on your chest? I don't know what the female equivalent is, but for us guys, our dads were forever telling us that doing this-or-that thing (that we didn't want to do) would be good for us. It would "put hair on your chest." Talk about a mixed blessing, right? They didn't tell us anything then about the repercussions of potentially having too much hair on our chests! But we want to do the hard thing! We want to impress our dads; we want to earn the hair on our chests! We have this innate desire to do things the hard way so that we can turn around, show off our metaphorically hairy chests, and say, "Look what I was able to do!" It's like Kennedy said: we climb the highest mountain, we sail across the sea. We go to the moon. All to prove ourselves. This is why we are suspicious about things that are given away for free or things that seem too easy. Must be junk, right? What can it possibly be worth if they're giving it away for nothing? You're always hearing this sentiment expressed in movies, aren't you? "Well, that was easy!" "Yeah," comes the inevitable and nervous reply, "*too* easy."

IS EASY WRONG?

Christians are the same way. We can't handle being given something for free, and certainly not if that thing is forgiveness, the love of God, and eternal life! We want desperately to earn it. We are like Naaman, incensed that our riches (our spiritual quality) and obedience are not required for our healing. If we can't earn our salvation, we think, we can at least struggle to retroactively purchase it by becoming people for whom a substitutionary sacrifice—the death of Jesus Christ on the cross—is not such a scandal. "Oh, so Jesus is gonna die for me is he?" we think. "Well, just wait until he sees what I'm gonna do for him!" We want to do something hard. We want to earn God's favor. We fear something easy, both because we don't understand it and because we've been convinced that something easy isn't worth anything. Naaman's servants point out the irony: if we were willing to do something difficult and expensive, something easy shouldn't offend us…rather, it should make us joyful! Having convinced ourselves that a righteous life is the path to God's love, the fact that God's love has been given to us for free on account of Christ should make us weep tears of joy, not frustration. However, frustration and suspicion often accompany things that seem too easy.

At the end of the 2016 film *Hail, Caesar!* (written by Joel and Ethan Coen), Eddie Mannix (Josh Brolin) sits in a confessional. Eddie is a studio fixer in the 1950s, a man whose job it is to take care of the studio's stars. He gets them out of scrapes with the law, solves pregnancy scares, squashes unflattering news stories, and the like. It's an exhausting job (the whole film takes place over the course of a single day), and Eddie's wondering if he should get out of the business that's wearing him down and causing him to go to confession multiple times per day. Complicating matters is a lucrative job offer from Lockheed which would allow Eddie more time with his family and a sense of having his feet planted more firmly in the real world—as opposed to Hollywood's dream factory...a factory of which Eddie is all too familiar with the seedy inner workings.

With all of this swirling around in his head, is it any wonder that Eddie asks the priest to whom he's confessing, "If there's something that's easy...is that wrong?" He's suspicious of the Lockheed job—of giving up the work that's driving him a little bit crazy—because he suspects that "taking the easy way out" is wrong *by definition*. He's resistant to what might be a better way forward for him because it is also an easy way forward.

In our devotional *It is Finished*, Tullian Tchividjian and I wrote that "our resistance to our no-cost salvation shows an ignorance of the most crucial tenant of our faith: while 'no pain, no gain' is quite true, the pain was suffered by another—a substitute, a savior—and need not continue. This easy thing, this free gift, is worth more than anything else in the world. Our pain, no gain. Jesus' pain, our gain—no charge."

CHAPTER 2

A LOGICAL IMPOSSIBILITY

In an April 2010 *Vanity Fair* essay called "The New Commandments," Christopher Hitchens and Jacques del Conte set out to "re-chisel" the 10 Commandments.[2] In the article, they go through the Exodus 20 list, as the subtitle suggests, "pruning the ethically dubious, challenging the impossible, and rectifying some serious omissions."

There is, as you might imagine, a lot that could be said about this project, but only one thing concerns me for the moment. It's a sentence that comes in the context of Hitchens and del Conte's discussion of the tenth commandment, "Thou shalt not covet thy neighbor's house, thou shalt not covet thy neighbor's wife, nor his manservant, nor his maidservant, nor his ox, nor his ass, nor anything that is thy neighbor's" (Exodus 20:17, KJV, version preserved from the article). After objecting to the way that the commandment seems to be addressed only "to the servant-owning and property-owning class," the authors turn to the content of the commandment itself. Here's what they say:

> Notice also that no specific act is being pronounced
> as either compulsory (the Sabbath) or forbidden

(perjury). Instead, this is the first but not the last introduction in the Bible of the totalitarian concept of "*thought crime*." You are being told, in effect, not even to think about it. (Jesus of Nazareth in the New Testament takes this a step further, announcing that those with lust in their heart have already committed the sin of adultery. In that case, you might as well be hung—or stoned—for a sheep as for a lamb, or for an ox or an ass if it cometh to that.) Wise lawmakers know that it is a mistake to promulgate legislation that is impossible to obey.

It's that last sentence that really catches the eye. On the face of it, this statement is inarguably true...but there's a huge logical fallacy at play here: Hitchens and del Conte assume that Almighty God is operating in the same way in which they see earthly lawmakers—wise or otherwise—operating! He's not. God uses the law in a completely unique way.

"Wise lawmakers," as the world understands them, use laws for basically one reason: to keep things in order. That's why there are things like stoplights, speed limits, and compulsory childhood education. Lawmakers want the world to work in an orderly and predictable way. It's also why murder and false testimony are illegal. You can't really have a functional society in which a person can just kill another person whenever they feel like it, and things would fall apart pretty quickly if people weren't compelled to tell the truth in legal matters. Thought of in this way, the use of the law is to inspire obedience. People, not knowing the good and right way to live life, need to be told. They need to be educated. They need to be forced to stop at red lights, to go to school, and to be honest. Once they get the proper information, the thinking goes, they'll know how to act in the world, and they'll do it. In this realm of law, a civil realm, Hitchens and del Conte are perfectly correct: it doesn't make any sense to make laws that are impossible to keep. But God is not from this realm, and he is doing something markedly different.

BOOTING COMPLIANCE

Recently, I saw a truck that made me break out into laughter in the middle of the street. No, it wasn't one of those Truly Nolen trucks with the mouse ears and tail. It was a truck from Premier Booting Services, one of those companies that comes to put the infernal metal lock on your front tire when you've parked illegally. So...that's not funny. It was actually their slogan that made me laugh: "Your Source for Parking Compliance." The way it was worded sounded like it came straight from the Ministry of Truth in George Orwell's *1984* or the identically-named organization from Terry Gilliam's *Brazil*. I laughed because, like the governments in those two stories, the slogan was using language to say the exact opposite of what the words meant.

Here's the irony of the slogan: Premier Booting Services doesn't actually *want* to provide parking compliance. That's the service they're advertising, but it is most decidedly not the service they intend to provide. In fact, successfully delivering "parking compliance" would put them out of business. In fact, Premier Booting Services depends on people not being compliant. They want people getting booted, and then getting booted again, on into infinity. People who learn their lesson and start parking legally actually become a problem for their business model! So, despite their advertising, Premier isn't actually in the compliance business; they're in the punishment business! They only say that they sell "compliance" because it doesn't sound as vicious.

This is how Christopher Hitchens and Jacques del Conte

are thinking about the law. In just the same way that Premier Booting Services promises "compliance," they claim that the application of the law to a situation should bring about obedience. Otherwise, what's the point? A Premier sales pitch—say, to the manager of an office building—might go something like, "A contract with Premier Booting services will ensure that no one illegally parks in your lot twice. Once someone is booted by us, they know better than to make that mistake again."

But remember, it's not actually in Premier Booting Services' best interest to provide compliance! A booting company doesn't want compliance; it actually *wants* violation. In the same way, the law doesn't actually bring about the obedience it desires. It can outline behavior that is compulsory or forbidden, but it cannot actually create the behavior. In fact, it normally creates the *opposite* behavior! In Romans 5, Paul creates a doublet that sheds light on the relationship between the law and obedience. It begins, "Now the law came in to increase the trespass..." (5:20a). Think about the feeling that blossoms within you when you're told that you're not allowed to do something. All of a sudden, you want to do it all the more. I have never wanted a cookie more than when I was forbidden to open the cookie jar.

When we think that telling bad people to be good—applying the boot to the tires of our spiritual lives—will actually produce compliance, we misunderstand the law's purpose, at least in God's eyes. We're *using* it incorrectly! The law makes us sin all the more! We would all agree, however, that compliance is a laudable goal. We want people parking legally and we want people living up to the standard that God has set for them. But how might we actually achieve compliance? Listen as Paul finishes his couplet: "...but where sin increased, grace abounded all the more" (Romans 5:20b).

Paul, when talking about an increasing trespass, doesn't double-down on the law. He goes the other way. When sin increases, grace abounds! The same counterintuitive thing happens when compliance is sought: against all human expectation, it is grace that produces compliance. It is only love that comes to you when you are undeserving that can change a heart, and it is only a changed heart that can bring forth true obedience. Punishment and judgment can modify behavior for a time, but they do so by creating a heart full of fear. This fearful heart will, in the end, not be obedient but rebellious. A truly reformed heart is created by love and grace. This reformed heart is a grateful one, which, contrary to the desires of a rebellious and fearful heart, actually desires to do whatever the lover asks.

So if the law doesn't produce compliance—if it's actually grace that produces compliance—then what is the law for? Here it is that we come to the unique way that God is using the law and why it actually makes completely logical sense for this "wise lawmaker…to promulgate legislation that is impossible to obey."

WE ASK, WE GET, WE DIE

There's an incredible passage buried in the book of Nehemiah (honestly, when was the last time you turned there during your quiet time?) that beautifully illustrates the way God uses the law. It's found at the beginning of Chapter 8. Here are a couple of excerpts:

> And all the people gathered as one man into the square before the Water Gate. And they told Ezra the scribe to bring the Book of the Law of Moses that the LORD had commanded Israel. So Ezra the priest brought the Law before the assembly, both men and women and all who could understand what they heard, on the first day of the seventh month. And he read from it facing the square before the Water Gate

> from early morning until midday, in the presence
> of the men and the women and those who could
> understand. And the ears of all the people were at-
> tentive to the Book of the Law...
>
> They read from the book, from the Law of God,
> clearly, and they gave the sense, so that the people
> understood the reading. And Nehemiah, who was
> the governor, and Ezra the priest and scribe, and
> the Levites who taught the people said to all the
> people, "This day is holy to the Lord your God; do
> not mourn or weep." For all the people wept as they
> heard the words of the Law. (1-3, 8-9)

The people of Israel have gathered together, and they've asked
Ezra to bring the book of the law and to read it to them. They
ask Ezra to bring the law. They think they want it. They want
to be told what to do. They want to learn. But then something
interesting happens: after this morning-long church service,
spent reading the book of the law and worshipping God, all the
people had broken down in tears. This is the way of life with
the law: we ask for it, we hear it, and when we understand it, we
are broken by it. This relationship with the law is as old as time
itself. We think we want it, but as soon as we get it, it kills us.

Why, then, do we ask for the law? You would think that
we'd want to be free, right? No rules, no restrictions. As Outback says, "No rules, just right." And that does sound pretty
great, in theory, but when we really get down to it, no rules or
restrictions means no way to tell who's better than anyone else.
And make no mistake, we are in love with determining who is
"better." In addition, we're convinced that the law will come in
and show everyone how well we're doing.

The Who have a greatest hits album called "Who's Better
Who's Best," and this is a great description of what we spend a
lot of our time doing: comparing ourselves to everyone around

us and trying to figure out where we rank. We think things like, "I may not be as good a father as Rick down the street who's always going to his kids' recitals, but I'm sure as heck a better father than Stan…that guy doesn't ever seem to be home at all!" The law, even though it might not be the kind of law that's written down anywhere, is what tells us what it means to be a good father, wife, daughter, brother, Christian… person! We are desperate to get credit for the good things we do, so we need there to be a structure to tell us what's good. That structure is the law. So we want it; we need it, because we need to know where we stand. Usually, though, we don't truly understand it.

It's clear that we don't understand it because we don't spend a lot of time like the Israelites did at the Water Gate. Remember, they spent the morning having the law read and interpreted to them, and by the end, they were totally wrecked. We, on the other hand, take a more active approach: in order to avoid becoming wreckage, we lower the standard or requirement of the law so that we can think of ourselves as having accomplished it.

Here's what I mean: When we hear the true standard, the full requirement, the real law, it destroys us. Far from showing us how well we're doing, the law shows us just how short we fall. Hitchens and del Conte nod to this when they note the apparent moral equivalence—as Jesus taught—of lust and adultery. No one can live up to the standard if the standard is "thought crime!" We are exactly like the Israelites in Nehemiah, destroyed by the realization that the law is beyond our ability to obey; that being a better father than Stan isn't good enough, that the standard is perfection (Matthew 5:48). We fall to our faces, covered in tears.

This is the first truth of true religion: the law will kill you. It will reduce you to tears and end your life. Even Indiana Jones (in *Raiders of the Lost Ark*) knew that he wasn't righteous enough to keep his eyes open when the Ark of the Covenant was opened. What did he know was in there? The law of God. He knew that the law would melt faces. So, if the law kills, what brings life? If the law destroys, what resurrects?

Ezra and Nehemiah tell the people not to be grieved, "for the joy of the LORD is your strength," even in this time when they feel so weak, so broken. "Now wait a minute!" you might say. "How can this God, whose law is so oppressive that it breaks his people down to tears and destroys our lives every day, also be our strength? Our protector? Our refuge?" In other words, how can the oncoming enemy force also be the rescuer? How can the judge also be the defense attorney?

The miracle of grace is this: law-maker is not God's only job description; or better, law is not the only thing God speaks. God is also and finally our savior, Jesus Christ. He doesn't just speak the law that puts sinners to death; he speaks the gospel that raises the dead. And he utters this second and final word at "just the right time." In Romans, we read that at just the right time, while we are ungodly, while we are sinners, Christ comes for us (5:6). He comes at the right time, while we are like the Israelites, oppressed by the law, on our faces under the weight of our own failures, covered in tears, and broken. Right then, Christ comes. As Jesus says in Luke: "The Spirit of the Lord is upon me, because he has anointed me to proclaim good news to the poor. He has sent me to proclaim liberty to the captives and recovering of sight to the blind, to set at liberty those who are oppressed, to proclaim the year of the Lord's favor" (4:18-19). Then he says, "Today this Scripture has been fulfilled in your hearing" (4:21).

The Good News of Jesus Christ, the Gospel that we preach, is that, though the law comes and destroys us, the Son of God comes and resurrects us. Our death is overturned by Christ's death. Our life is created by Christ's life. We hear the law and we are brought to tears. We hear the Gospel and we are moved to joy. In Christ, we who were poor are now rich. We who were captive are now released. We who were blind now can see. We who were oppressed now are free. We who were dead are now alive. In Christ, this is the year of the Lord's favor. Today, even as you read these words, is the day of the Lord's favor, achieved by Jesus, for you.

THE BAR ALWAYS WINS

I was a high jumper in high school. I only did it for the spring track season of my senior year, because I was cut from the base-ball team. I am tall though, and as a basketball player, had always been an above-average jumper. In other words, I was better than I really had any business being—having not ever done it before—but not nearly as well-trained as anyone else I was jumping against. This led to a dangerously over-developed self-confidence.

A high jump competition is at least partially about psychology. It helps to psych yourself up for the competition, and it helps just as much to psych out your opponents. If a jumper didn't feel like they could beat me, I felt like they would knock the bar down early in the competition—failing psychologically before they failed physically. One way that I would try to intimidate my opponents was during warm-ups, by standing stock still at the bar (without the customary run-up) and jumping over what I thought were impressive heights. Another way to try to psych out opponents was to leave my sweats on and "pass" multiple lower heights—to not even deign to begin competing until the bar was at an impressive level. As long as you clear a height, it doesn't matter whether you did or didn't clear any lower heights—every jumper is judged by the highest height cleared. As I said "pass" at each height, the other jumpers would look over—or so I thought—and think to themselves, "Wow…he must be really good!"

At one particular meet, though, I overdid it. I passed on too many heights. By the time I made my first attempt, the bar was set at a height that I'd only cleared a couple of times. I made my three attempts, and I knocked the bar down every time. I ended the competition with no height cleared and in last place.

As I reflect on that experience, as painful as it was, something profound occurs to me: I knocked down the bar three times. The winner knocked down the bar three times. I failed at the beginning, he failed at the end. In a high jump competition, the winner is just the person who fails last. The bar wins every time. As humiliated as I felt clearing no heights in the competition, I was simply being brought up against my limitations. The competition's winner felt the same friction: the limits of his physical ability pressing up against that unyielding standard of the bar.

In *Cast Away*, Tom Hanks plays a FedEx executive who gets stranded on a desert island. Long before the island, however, he's trying to motivate a group of package sorters in Russia. He points to a clock counting down the remaining time until a delivery truck leaves their plant and says, "Time rules over us without mercy, not caring if we're healthy or ill, hungry or drunk, Russian or American or beings from Mars. It's like a fire; it can either destroy us or it can keep us warm. That's why every FedEx office has a clock. Because we live or we die by the clock. We never turn our back on it, and we never ever allow ourselves the sin of losing track of time…that's how much time we have before this pulsating, accursed, relentless taskmaster tries to put us out of business."

This is how God is using the law: as a pulsating, accursed, relentless taskmaster charged with putting us out of business. In Romans 3:20, Paul writes that "By works of the law no human being will be justified in [God's] sight, since through the law comes knowledge of sin." In other words, no one will become obedient by trying to obey the law. That's not the law's purpose. The law is being used by God to bring knowledge of sin. Like the unforgiving high jump bar—which just keeps getting higher and higher—the law brings people into contact with their limitations.

No one defeats the high jump bar. It's impossible. The bar simply gets raised until the last competitor fails to clear it. God intends his law to accomplish the same feat: to show people their failure and their need for a savior. This is the wisdom of the truly "wise lawmaker." He has made his law impossible to keep in order to shine a light on his Son, the one who actually did keep it.

But like I did, we refuse to consider the bar impossible to clear. We look at it, leave our sweats on, and think, "That shouldn't be a problem; I can do better than that." We spend our lives looking at things that are impossible and convincing ourselves that they are merely difficult. We couldn't be more wrong.

CHAPTER 3

MISSION: DIFFICULT

I have heard the Christian life described in many different ways. Some have compared it to a race, or a job, or a train trip, or any number of other things. But the description of the Christian life that has stuck with me for the longest was one offered by my friend Jono Linebaugh (he's now Dr. Jonathan A. Linebaugh…but back then, he was just Jono) in a Mission and Evangelism class in seminary. He gave this description as part of a personal testimony: the Christian life, he said, was like a mountain surrounded by a gated fence. The goal is to get to the top of the mountain, to be close to God. The Good News about Jesus Christ, Jono said, was that he had come from heaven to earth—come down the mountain—to open the gate in the fence. It was then up to the Christian, through hard work and dedication, to climb to the top of the mountain, to get to God.

This was exactly the idea of the Christian life I had grown up with: Jesus gets you in, but it's up to you to improve your standing. In Jono's defense, he went on to say that though he had grown up with this picture of Christianity, he had come to understand that this wasn't the true Gospel. I mean, after all, didn't Jesus say, "Take my yoke upon you, and learn from me, for I am gentle and lowly in heart, and you will find rest for your souls. For my yoke is easy, and my burden is light" (Matthew 11:29-30)? How often I had considered those words and wondered at how falsely they rang. My early Christian life did not seem easy, nor my burden light. In fact, Jesus seemed to have added burdens to my life! Now, as a Christian, I needed to be careful about my language, the kinds of movies I watched, the music I listened to, the politicians with whom I agreed, and on and on. I had worried about none of these things before I became a Christian. And popular Christian culture didn't seem to be doing me any favors either.

You've heard things like "God helps those who help themselves," right? And "God will go ninety-nine yards if you just go one"? Or "Jesus is a gentleman"? There's also a famous painting called *The Light of the World* by William Holman Hunt that depicts Jesus about to knock on a door that's covered in vines, having clearly gone unopened for years. Tellingly, Hunt has painted no knob on Jesus' side of the door…it must be opened from the inside. Jesus is just waiting on you to do one little thing (open the door) so that he can come in and do all of the required housecleaning. All of these cultural touchstones put the pressure on the Christian to do the climbing of Jono's metaphorical mountain. But notice who has to do the hard work! It's you! You're still the one who has to climb the mountain. It all depends on you. Think about it: if God helps those who help themselves, then the whole system depends on you helping yourself. Only then can (or will) God step in and help you. Even if God is willing to go ninety-nine yards, he is paralyzed until you go your one. Again, the whole system depends on you. If Jesus is a gentleman, then the whole system depends on you inviting him in. If there's no knob on Jesus' side of the door, the whole system depends on you undoing the latch. Do you hear the refrain? It seemed to me that, as I heard it normally discussed in the Christian culture, the whole system depended on me. God was ready to do his part, but I had to do mine first. That yoke is not easy. That burden is not light.

Saving yourself is impossible. I think that most Christian people would say that. But "helping" yourself, and counting on God to do the rest? That just sounds difficult. Going one hundred yards is impossible. But going one yard, and counting on God to do the rest? That sounds doable. Unlocking the door for a gentleman Jesus sounds doable too. If the impossible is rare, and the difficult is common, then the whole system depends on you. And make no mistake: a system that depends on you is terrible news.

CHECKING OUT

On their 2011 self-titled debut album, The Belle Brigade has a really catchy song called "Losers." The first lines are pretty powerful:

> There will always be someone better than you
> Even if you're the best
> So let's stop the competition now
> Or we will both be losers
> And I'm ashamed I ever tried to be higher than the
> rest
> But brother I am not alone
> We've all tried to be on top of the world somehow,
> 'Cause we have all been losers

The song is about something impossible. The Belle Brigade is acknowledging the inevitable failure-by-comparison of human life, the constant feeling of losing that seems to naturally accompany being a person in this world. The law, they're saying, is real. And it hurts. Despite the accuracy of their diagnosis, though, the Belle Brigade's prescription falls well short of the mark:

So I wanna make it clear now
I wanna make it known
That I don't care about any of that [expletive] no
    more
Don't care about being a winner
Or being smooth with women
Or going out on Fridays
Being the life of parties
No, no more, no

So, the answer to the impossibilities of life is to...stop caring? To check out? How exactly does one do that? I desperately wish I could just declare myself immune from the law's demand: I will *not* feel that I have to be a better provider for my family than I am. I will *not* let others' expectations rule (and subsequently destroy) my life. I will *not* worry that everyone in my life is about to realize that I'm not worth their attention.

Sadly, the law's demands on us weigh heavily whether we accept them or not. Whether we acknowledge them or not. Whether we believe in them or not. Their truth is undeniable: I want to be a winner. I want to be smooth with women. I want to go out on Fridays. I'm desperate to be the life of parties.

The law is the hurricane that threatens to rip our house from its foundation. Facing the wind and screaming, "I don't believe in your power! You will not destroy my house!" is a fool's errand. The wind is there—and devastating—whether you believe in it or not. This is The Belle Brigade doing its best Anthony Hopkins and sending us out on a Mission: Difficult. But it's not a walk in the park...because it's not difficult. It turns out that this mission—this life—actually *is* impossible. It turns out that it's best to acknowledge the law's power to destroy—to realize the impossibility of overcoming it—and to get a new house, a place prepared for us by Christ (John 14:2).

AN ASTRONAUT AND A SWIMMER

Billy Bob Thornton made a little movie in 2006 called *The Astronaut Farmer*. It's the kind of movie you can get for $1.99 in a bargain bin at a record store. You know the kind of movie I mean. Thornton plays Charles Farmer, an ex-NASA astronaut who builds a rocket in his barn. He never got to go into space as an official astronaut, so his plan is to do it under his own power (literally). Everything is going well, and no one is the wiser... until he tries to buy 50,000 gallons of high-test rocket fuel over the Internet. Both the FBI and the FAA get involved, worried that he might be building a weapon or setting a seriously worrying new precedent in space flight.

At the FAA hearing to discuss his flight plan (which was originally ignored as a prank), Farmer stands up and makes a stirring speech:

> You see, when I was a kid they used to tell me that I could be anything I wanted to be. No matter what. And maybe I am insane... I don't know...but I still believe that. I believe with all my heart. Somewhere along the line we stopped believing that we could do anything. And if we don't have our dreams, we have nothing.

Now, this kind of sentiment is held close to the human heart. Truth be told, though? It totally rubs me the wrong way. Worse than that is the fact that it's just not true. There are a host of other examples, the most ridiculous of which are the many professional athletes who claim that their recent championship is proof that "you can do anything you set your mind to." I remember a time when Michael Phelps, the 23-time Olympic gold medalist, was interviewed after stepping out of the pool following one of his gold medal wins. His said something like, "It just proves that if you want something enough, you can do anything." This is, to my mind, absurd. Did the other swimmers simply want the victory less than Phelps did? Would someone with a shorter wingspan, smaller muscles, and less ability to hold their breath underwater be able to beat Phelps, as long as their desire was sufficient?

You'll hear this, too, when sports announcers suggest that a player has "willed" his team to victory, when, in point of fact, he has simply played better than the opponent. A more accurate phrase would be that he has "talented" his team to victory... but we desperately want to give the credit to our wills, because it means that things are difficult (anyone can accomplish this thing if they want it badly enough) and not impossible (no one but the genetically gifted physical freaks who play professional sports can do what just happened). But let's not get ahead of ourselves; we'll talk more about the will in Chapter 6.

The Christian intersection is this: the more capable we feel as humans, the less likely we are to admit to a need for a savior. The theological way to put this is that as one's anthropology (view of humanity) rises, one's Christology (view of Christ) falls. If it were true that God helped those who help themselves, then hard work and strong belief would be necessary ingredients to a Christian life. But, thank God, that phrase is not found anywhere in the Bible. By contrast, Jesus consistently seemed to go to those who could not help themselves: the lame, the sick, even the dead. He even went so far as to make his mission to the helpless explicit: "Those who are well have no need of a physician, but those who are sick. I came not to call the righteous, but sinners" (Mark 2:17). It is good news, indeed, for those of us who can't do just anything we set our minds to, or even get through an average day in our very average lives, that God helps the helpless. The first step to understanding that Good News, then, is to *admit* that you're helpless—what the church has traditionally called "confession"—and that "you can do anything you set your mind to" is just a platitude. As the saying goes, the first step is admitting you've got a problem. As we'll see in the next chapter, that's God's first goal with his revelation to us: to convince us that our situation is bad enough to warrant a savior. God's second goal, as we'll further see, is to assure us—and sinners everywhere—that our savior has come.

CHAPTER 4

IMPOSSIBLE IN SCRIPTURE

Remember Christopher Hitchens and Jacques del Conte's argument from Chapter 2, that no wise lawmaker would promulgate legislation that is impossible to obey? We've seen how God uses the law in a different way than Hitchens and del Conte are used to, to show people their need for a savior instead of simply to inspire obedience. Now we'll see that "legislation"—laws, rules, regulations—are not the only impossible things in the world that God has made. As I've said, impossible is everywhere. In the next chapter, we'll discuss the impossible in everyday life, but for now, let's turn our eyes to the impossible as it exists in God's word.

A MIRACLE, SOAKING WET (1 KINGS 18:20-39)

Elijah is frustrated with the people of Israel. They're in the land of the Canaanites, "limping between two different opinions" (1 Kings 18:21), going back and forth between following the God who rescued them from their captivity in Egypt and following Baal, the deity of the local people. Elijah finally throws down the gauntlet with the prophets of Baal in an effort to prove to the people that Baal is no god at all, that only the God of their fathers—Abraham, Isaac, and Jacob—is the one true God. In order to show the people who the *real* God is, he sets up a test. He tells the gathered crowd that he and the prophets of Baal will each set up an altar, get a bull, and prepare everything for the sacrifice…but they'll stop short of completing the ceremony. Then, they'll each call on their god to light the sacrifice on fire. Whichever god lights the sacrifice will be worshipped as the true God.

The prophets of Baal go first, getting everything prepared. They call upon the name of their god, but nothing happens. They even go so far as to "cut themselves after their custom with swords and lances, until the blood gushed out upon them" (18:28). They try all day to get Baal to send fire to light their offering. Scripture says, "No one answered; no one paid attention" (18:29). Now it's Elijah's turn. Instead of merely asking God to send fire from the heavens to light his sacrifice on fire, Elijah calls for his altar to be completely drenched in water first…and not only that, but drenched three times (18:33-35)!

Elijah is moving this act of God from difficult to impossible. To our modern ears, this might not make much sense, but on the ground in those days it was perfectly reasonable. A god might well be expected to answer the cries of his people to light a sacrifice on fire…but not on an altar upon which fire could not burn. Elijah is proving to the people not only that the God of Abraham, Isaac, and Jacob exists, but that he is the God of the impossible. He can not only send fire from heaven, but his fire will be powerful enough to consume a soaked altar, the stones that surround it, and "[lick] up the water that was in the trench." The Israelites' response is appropriate: "They fell on their faces and said, 'The LORD, he is God; the LORD, he is God'" (18:38-39). If God had merely sent fire when Baal couldn't, he might have been nothing more than a better, more powerful god than Baal. A God who can consume a thrice-soaked altar? He is almighty God, Lord of the impossible.

AN IMPOSSIBLE REQUEST (GENESIS 22:1-14)

The command that Abraham sacrifice his son Isaac is, for many people, the thing about God that they can't get past. "Yes," we find ourselves saying, "God has done all manner of wonderful things for humankind…but this is monstrous. Asking a man to sacrifice his own son? Such a god does not deserve our worship."

It's made worse, too, that the story is presented as a test— God testing Abraham to examine the quality of his faith. It seems all the more callous that this awful request is made just to see how solid Abraham's faith is. It's true that, when Abraham's faith proves worthy, a substitute sacrifice is provided. But that's the end of the story. For now, let's focus on the beginning.

God comes to Abraham and asks for the impossible. But as we've seen, and as we'll continue to see, this is not extraordinary. God asks for the impossible all the time. He asks you to turn the other cheek (Matthew 5). He asked the rich young man to give away all of his possessions (Mark 10). He asks that you be truly content (1 Timothy 6). Finally, and with perhaps the greatest kick in the teeth, he asks that you be perfect, just as he is perfect (Matthew 5:48).

But Abraham's God, though he asks the impossible, loves accomplishing it. When Isaac asks his father where the lamb for the burnt offering is (he can see the wood and the fire), Abraham says, "God will provide for himself the lamb for a burnt offering, my son." After arriving at the top of the mountain where the sacrifice was to take place, Abraham "reached out his hand and took the knife to slaughter his son." After an angel of the Lord stops him, Abraham lifts his eyes and finds a ram, caught in a thicket. God has indeed provided the lamb for the burnt offering, and it is not Abraham's son. So Abraham gives the place a name: he calls it "The LORD will provide." Notice that he doesn't call it "The Quality of My Faith." It's not the faith of Abraham that was meant to be remembered, it is the faithfulness of God to provide: "As it is said to this day, 'On the mount of the LORD it shall be provided'" (Genesis 22:14).

The story of Abraham and Isaac isn't just a quirk of history, a profound myth to help us understand the importance of faith. Abraham's almost-sacrifice of his son is the deepest proof of what is God's deepest truth: He asks for the impossible, and then provides.

St. Paul puts forth an interesting dichotomy in Romans: "Let not sin therefore reign in your mortal body, to make you obey its passions" (6:12) and "thanks be to God, that you who were once slaves of sin…have become slaves of righteousness" (6:17-18). Paul asks for the impossible: do not let sin control you. And then he proclaims the work accomplished: you have been set free.

This is what the story of Abraham and Isaac is really about. A man asked to show his righteousness—his faith—in the most impossible way: the sacrifice of a son. When the moment comes, God provides another way: a ram, caught in the thicket. This story is our story too. Whenever we are asked to prove ourselves to God, to live up to the standard that he has set for us, we fall short. All of our shortfalls, though, are caught up in one moment, a final moment, at an ultimate time, and God provides another way. He sacrifices his son, and we are set free. Unlike Abraham, God actually goes through with it. So we called this place, the mountaintop of our lives, "The Lord will provide"; and we proclaim it to this day: On the mount of the Lord, Jesus paid the price for the sins of the world.

THE AMAZING SHRINKING ARMY (JUDGES 6-7)

God knows how desperately we want to take credit for accomplishments. What's difficult is to give others credit when they deserve it. It's especially difficult when that "other" is the unseen God of the universe, if it is only by his power that we can do anything at all. I've heard it said that God is in the idol-destruction business...which sounds okay until we realize that our most precious idol is our own self-sufficiency. God, though, knows that it's this most precious idol that is most in need of destruction. The story of Gideon and his 300-man army is a perfect illustration of this idol-destroying work of God.

Judges 6 opens like many other chapters in the book: the people of Israel have again "whored after other gods" and again the Lord has seen their wicked behavior and has raised up a nation through which Israel will feel his judgment. The Midianites are especially vicious, and have brought God's people as low as they ever have been—they're hiding out in mountain caves and are carrying out even their normal daily business in secret. For instance, Gideon harvests wheat in his winepress so the Midianites won't find out about it. So how will Gideon come up against the oppressive Midianites when his judgeship is finally ready to be exercised? We might expect Gideon to engage extra recruits, forge more weapons, and concoct special tactics to come against such a fearsome fighting force. But that's not God's plan for Gideon and his people. Gideon's army isn't going to be fortified. In fact, it's going to be reduced.

Gideon begins with what probably already seemed like a paltry number—32,000 men—and ends up with only 300. Oh, and it's not as if the 300 who remained were 300 highly trained, black-belt ninjas, chosen for their skill in the deadly arts. They weren't the 300 men of Sparta who defended Thermopylae. No, the criterion used to isolate the final 300 must have seemed like a joke: did the soldier kneel down and put his mouth to the water, or did he scoop a handful up and lap it like a dog? The lappers, Scripture says, "prevailed." That is, of course, if you define "prevailing" as having to fight in a woefully undermanned army against the ruthless occupying force. Oh, and don't forget: these soldiers who "prevailed" have to fight this fight with trumpets and torches instead of swords and shields. But remember the lesson of Isaac's sacrifice and Elijah's altar: God turns the difficult into the impossible to show how powerful he is.

In 1 Corinthians, St. Paul said that "God chose what is foolish in the world to shame the wise" and that "God chose what is weak in the world to shame the strong" (1:27). Here, God has made the Israelites both weak (by reducing their numbers) and foolish (by taking away their weapons and giving them musical instruments). God tells Gideon exactly why he reduced his fighting force: "The people with you are too many for me to give the Midianites into their hand, lest Israel boast over me, saying, 'My own hand has saved me'" (Judges 7:2). God is *making* his people see their need for a savior.

A while ago, a dear friend posted a photo on Instagram that piqued my interest immediately. It showed her son, wearing a *gi*, proudly holding up a broken board. Her caption said, "Joel the white belt." Now, as proud as I am about my dear friend's kid's achievements, this wasn't what drew my attention. The board, though split down the middle, had "Good job!" written on it. It also had Joel's name, the date, and the name of the Grand Master who, I assume, oversaw the accomplishment. Here's the fascinating thing, though: *the words were written across the break.* In other words, the Grand Master had written "Good job!" on the board *before* Joel successfully broke it!

My mind immediately went to God, because this is exactly how he operates. It's what he did with Gideon! "That same night the LORD said to him, 'Arise, go down against the camp, for I have given it into your hand'" (Judges 7:9). Notice the tense of God's announcement to Gideon: God is telling Gideon to begin the fight against the Midianites and is—at the same time—telling him that the battle is already won! He's not merely promising victory (as he would have been had he said "and I *will* give it into your hand"); he's telling him that the fight is *actually already over.*

Our Grand Master has written "Good job!" on the board before he asks his child to break it. This is how the grace of God works, accomplishing a thing and then attributing it to the undeserving. In Romans 5, Paul tells us that God comes to people while they are sinners, before they are righteous, and yes, even while they are his enemies. God calls the children that he has adopted in Christ "righteous" before they become so. This is the beauty of imputation: "For our sake he made [Jesus] to be sin who knew no sin, so that in him we might become the righteousness of God" (2 Corinthians 5:21). God calls a sinner righteous on account of Christ, and the sinner is made righteous, outside of any earning, deserving, or achievement.

Ordinary human life doesn't work this way. In our economy, you get what you earn. You hoist the trophy after you win the championship. The Marine Corps sword is "always earned, never given." The Bachelor contestant gets the rose after she impresses the man on the date. You get the promotion at work after you've shown your earning power. The Grand Master gives you the "good job" after you break the board. But not in God's dojo.

God comes to us first. He comes to the weak, to the foolish, to the powerless. He comes to the sinner and to the rebel. In fact, he comes to the dead! It's not just that we're too weak to break the board on our own…we are actually "dead in our trespasses and sins" (Ephesians 2:1), unable to lift our arms at all.

God's first work is to show us our true state. We are loath to admit weakness, much less death, so sometimes, he lets us whack away at the board for a while. It hurts. We hit the board hard, because we'd love to be able to say what God knew the Israelites would say: "My own hand has saved me." So God takes us down a notch. Or a couple. Or the number-of-notches equivalent of 31,700 warriors. Gideon's tiny army would have felt like dead men as they walked down to Midian's encampment.

The bad news is tough to take: you can't win this fight. But the good news is great: this fight has already been won on your behalf! This is what the David and Goliath story is all about (1 Samuel 17). David's victory over the Philistines is credited to the cowardly Israelite army, who never even have to take up arms!

We Christians know the Good News, that the victory is already won, but we all too often forget it. We forget, as we bloody our knuckles on that board, that Jesus hung on the cross and shouted, "It is finished!" Sin and death have been defeated; Christ's righteousness has been given to you.

In God's economy, the trophy is presented before the competition and the rose is given before the date. "Good job"—or "Well done, good and faithful servant"—is already written on our board. The pressure's off; the victory is won. The victor, Jesus Christ, has given his victory to us. The board is already broken. Unlike the Marine Corps sword, God's love is never earned, and is always given.

BETWEEN THE WAVES (EXODUS 14)

Having only recently felt the freedom of having escaped from slavery in Egypt, God's people are trapped. A huge sea is in front of them, a giant desert is all around them, and an enormous army commanded by an angry Pharaoh is bearing down on them. There seems to literally be no way out but death, and they complain to Moses that it would have been better for them to have been left in punishing slavery in Egypt than to face the fate that is before them now. But the God of the impossible is just about to get to work. "The LORD said to Moses, 'Why do you cry to me? Tell the people of Israel to go forward. Lift up your staff, and stretch out your hand over the sea and divide it, that the people of Israel may go through the sea on dry ground'" (Exodus 14:15-16).

God doesn't send his people around the Red Sea. He doesn't arrange it so that a great fleet shows up in the nick of time. He doesn't bring them out of Egypt by any difficult route. He brings them out of Egypt by an impossible route: through the midst of a sea, but on dry ground. As we have seen time and again in Scripture, this is the way the God of Abraham, Isaac, and Jacob works. There are countless more examples—some of which we will look at later in this book—of the God of creation seemingly circumventing the natural rules of that creation to achieve his purposes. Our God delights in accomplishing the impossible. This is good news indeed.

CHAPTER 5

IMPOSSIBLE IN LIFE

I think I first became aware of the impossible in my life—at least aware enough that it kicked off a sort of mini existential crisis—when my wife and I were approaching the birth of our first child. I realized, as the date came closer and closer, that I was becoming more and more nervous and agitated. I'd never been a father before, and I wasn't sure I could be a good one. In fact, I wasn't sure what to do at all! The choices seemed endless: cloth diapers or disposable? Jarred food or blend-your-own? Breast milk or formula? Spanking or not? Harvard or Yale? In all seriousness, though, the decision tree that spread out before me was tremendous—never-ending, actually—and it was stressing me out. It wasn't until later that I realized what was actually going on. It turned out that I was subconsciously convinced—in a way that I never would have admitted consciously—that if I made all the right choices along that infinite parenting decision tree, that my child would grow up to be Chief Justice of the Supreme Court or the next Oprah Winfrey. You'll say, of course, that such a thought is ridiculous…and of course you're right. But we all think this way, all the time. Most of the stress in our lives comes from the fact that we've convinced ourselves—often only subconsciously—that the sum of our decision-making will determine how well things turn out for us. Who wouldn't feel stressed? In that scheme, your happy future depends on every minute-by-minute choice that you make! What finally gave me some peace, and the ability to approach the birth of our daughter with some mental stability, was the realization that making all the right decisions along the parenting decision tree was impossible. Not difficult, impossible. It wasn't something that I could buckle down on, or something I could solve with parenting books or daddy blogs… there was no way to make my way through unscathed. No, I had to acknowledge from the very beginning that failure was my sure destination. "Success," as I had subconsciously defined it, was impossible. Ironically and counterintuitively, it was in admitting failure that I found peace.

This is beautifully illustrated by a first-season episode of *Frasier* called "Selling Out." Frasier—a radio psychiatrist—is offered the opportunity to make some extra money by personally endorsing products on the air. First a Chinese restaurant, and then a hot tub company. Seeking to maintain his medical ethics, he refuses. Then, enticed by the amount of money he's been offered, he agrees, on the condition that he try and like the products that he is endorsing.

Before long, the Holy Grail of endorsements is offered: doing ads on television. This throws him back into a quandary. He doesn't especially like the product (snack nuts), and the commercial includes a blow to his ego (he must pop out of a giant foam peanut shell). As is his custom, he goes to his brother, a psychiatrist in private practice, for advice. Here's how the exchange plays out:

> FRASIER: "I'm afraid that I'm compromising my integrity as a psychiatrist."
>
> NILES: "I don't see this as a problem."

FRASIER: "You don't think this is the selling-out of Frasier Crane?"

NILES, laughing: "Oh, certainly not! You sold out a long time ago. The moment you agreed to do that call-in show you sold out."

FRASIER: "Niles, you are such a purist. Granted, I can't do the kind of in-depth analysis one can with a single patient, but my show literally helps thousands of people a day!"

NILES: "Let's face it, Frasier. You talk about wanting to safeguard your professional dignity, but the first time you went on the air you got out of medicine and into show-biz."

Niles then likens Frasier's show to an actress who did a nude scene and then complained that no one took her seriously as an artist. Disappointed, Frasier asks, "So what you're saying is that I shouldn't do it?"

"No, no, no," concludes Niles. "I'm saying it doesn't matter. Let's face it, Frasier. They've already looked up your skirt and seen everything there is to see."

The Christian version of my fatherhood conundrum is a similar decision tree: at each fork we imagine that sin lies down one path and righteousness down the other. If we can make all the right choices, everything will be fine. St. Paul had a different perspective, and it shows why I could find peace through acknowledging failure. Paul asked, "How can we who died to sin still live in it?" (Romans 6:2). He's not telling the Romans *not* to sin; he's saying that they're incapable of it! He's with Niles! Frasier *can't* lose his medical ethics! They're already gone! So what does Frasier do? Knowing that he has the freedom, having already been "outed" as a "sinner" by Niles, does he shoot the smarmy snack nut commercial? Does he think, "Well, I've breached my ethics, might as well keep breaching them"? No. Repentance sets him free. Dr. Joyce Brothers shoots the ad. Freedom in the Gospel does not create license, as so many fear. Counterintuitively, it creates the thing that ethics, that the law, wanted in the first place: righteousness. Acknowledging the impossibility of life does not produce paralysis and depression, it produces freedom and peace.

LITTLE LEAGUE AND A LIONS' DEN

In the qualifying rounds of the 2012 Little League World Series, a team from Petaluma, California, defeated a team from Nanakuli, Hawaii, by appealing a play at third. In short, a Hawaiian runner missed third on his way to score the tying run in the final inning, and was called out after the play when Petaluma appealed, ending the game. In his article on Yahoo Sports about the game, Cameron Smith said that the California squad reached the World Series "in the most controversial of circumstances." This would be incredible hyperbole under normal circumstances (there was no doping, game-throwing, or puberty-reaching, all of which would have been more controversial), but here, it's even more out of place: Petaluma won the game according to the rules! Touching all of the bases is pretty fundamental to baseball, and appeal plays exist for just this sort of circumstance.

The "controversy" in this story is largely due to the heart-breaking nature of Nanakuli's loss. They got the hits required to win the game but lost on a "technicality." Shouldn't the Petaluma coach have forgone the appeal and let the Hawaiians win? Wouldn't that have been the gracious thing to do?

Before we answer that question, though, let's look for a moment at the story about Daniel and the lions' den. In Daniel 6, Darius is tricked into making a law that will necessarily find his trusted advisor Daniel in violation: all of Darius' subjects must pray only to the king, and not to any god. Daniel, of course, being faithful, prays to God and is summarily found to be guilty of breaking the law. The penalty for breaking this law is a night in the lions' den. So Daniel is thrown to the lions. This always bothered me a great deal. Hasn't the king just made that law? Can't he change it back, or at least make an exception for Daniel? And yes, I know that "it is a law of the Medes and Persians that no injunction or ordinance that the king establishes can be changed" (6:15), but…come on. This is a king we're talking about here!

But here's the thing: changing the law would ruin the story! One of the great misconceptions about Christianity is that grace involves setting aside, circumventing, or ignoring the rules (the law). Upon hearing this Little League World Series story, a part of my heart thought, "Wouldn't it have been a wonderful example of grace if Petaluma, though knowing about the infraction, conceded the game to Nanakuli anyway?" But do you know what? It wouldn't have been. Grace doesn't mean playing the game as though there aren't any rules. Though grace does imply "unmerited favor," it carries with it the assumption of substitution, the game-changing fact that someone else has followed the rules in our stead.

Life without the law makes as little sense as a baseball game in which base-touching is optional. The law is never optional, and grace and the Gospel cannot forget about the law. In fact, it is the law that makes us aware of our need for the Gospel (Romans 7:7)! Our lives, and our faith, make sense when we understand that the rules haven't been done away with, they have instead been fulfilled for us (Matthew 5:18). God, we are told, will not be mocked (Galatians 6:7); his law is holy, righteous and good, and must be upheld. All the bases must be touched for the run to count. Thank God, though, that all the bases laid out before us have been touched by the one, Christ Jesus, who is holy, righteous and good, when we cannot be. The Gospel is not that Daniel doesn't have to go to the lions...the Gospel is that God is his rescuer *in the lions' den*!

EARN THIS

An old man, James Ryan walks through the American Cemetery in Normandy. He stops at a headstone and falls to his knees, tears in his eyes. The headstone reads "John Miller." As Ryan's wife comes to his side, he says through his tears, "Have I been a good man? Tell me I've lived a good life." Moved, his wife assures Ryan that he has. Yet the tears don't abate. James Ryan can't be sure if he's been good enough.

In *Saving Private Ryan*, Steven Spielberg marshals a wonderful ensemble cast to tell a wonderfully scripted, beautifully shot, movingly acted, and soul-crushingly judgmental story. John Miller (Tom Hanks) is tasked with taking a squad of eight men to find just one. Private James Ryan is the fourth son of a woman who has lost the other three in World War II. It has been decided that she will not lose a fourth. Miller's squad eventually loses almost every man in the effort to save Private Ryan.

Miller meets his own end defending a bridge by Ryan's side. With his last breath, he looks at Private Ryan and whispers, "Earn this." With these words, he dies. We flash sixty years into the future, and the octogenarian Ryan has clearly lived his entire life with this great weight on his shoulders. Has he indeed earned the salvation that Miller's squad gave their lives for? Miller himself, earlier in the film, muses, "He better be worth it. He'd better go home and cure a disease, or invent a longer-lasting light bulb." Has he discovered a cure for malaria? Has he invented cold fusion? That awesome upside-down ketchup bottle? As viewers, we aren't given to know. What we do know, however, is that he's worried. Why else does he beseech his wife to comfort him? We see that he has a beautiful family. His wife tells him he has been a good man. Clearly, leading a good life has not freed him from the judgment of Miller's words.

Christians too often hear these words, "Earn this," coming from Jesus' lips as he dies on the cross. We hear sermons to this effect: "Is the life you're living worth the death he died?" We live our lives trying to earn it, to become someone for whom such a sacrifice isn't so radically inappropriate. We turn into old James Ryans, worried that it hasn't been quite enough. The most shocking revelation of the film is that Ryan's wife has no idea who John Miller is! Miller's judgment has been so heavy that Ryan has not been able to share his name or story with his beloved for his whole life!

But Jesus doesn't say, "Earn this" from the cross. He says, "It is finished." Even more radically, he says, "I tell the truth, today you will be with me in paradise." The message of the Gospel is diametrically opposed to John Miller's "Earn this." Miller applies the law to Ryan's future in a way that Ryan can never escape. No matter how profound an altruist Ryan may become, the profundity of Miller's sacrifice will never allow Ryan to feel satisfied, or safe from Miller's judgment-from-beyond-the-grave. One word of law destroys the grace Miller shows in sacrificing his life for Ryan. But it is not so with Christ.

No word of law escapes Christ's lips from the cross. Incredibly, the word and weight of the law is applied to Christ ("My God, my God, why have you forsaken me?"). We are freed, and safe. We don't feel compelled to hide what Jesus has done for us, as Ryan hid what Miller did for him, because Jesus expects nothing of us. Our Savior doesn't say, "Earn this." He says, "It is finished...you will be with me in paradise."

THE CORNER OF MY EYES

One of the issues that Christian men all seem to deal with is lust. Bundles of books have been written to give men the tools they need to avoid this besetting sin. Indeed, no man can read Jesus' words on lust in the Sermon on the Mount without wincing: "You have heard that it was said, 'You shall not commit adultery.' But I say to you that everyone who looks at a woman with lustful intent has already committed adultery with her in his heart" (Matthew 5:27-28). I remember flipping through a popular Christian book and coming across the author's anecdote about female joggers. This man had found that he had a particular problem lusting after female joggers on the side of the road. He found that, as he drove his car, his eyes were inexorably drawn to these women. His counsel to the reader was to try what had worked for him: keep your eyes on the road. He'd found, he claimed, that if he was vigilant about keeping his eyes straight ahead, and could only see these women in his peripheral vision, he didn't lust. He couldn't lust, in other words, out of the corners of his eyes.

Now, let me be clear: I'm glad that this strategy worked for him, and I encourage all men to do whatever they can to avoid objectifying and lusting after women. But I can only wish that such a strategy could work for me. Perhaps it's just that I'm better at lusting than this author, but I've found that I don't even need my eyes to be open to fall into lust! My thoughts alone are sinful enough, thank you very much...no eyes required! Lust is not merely a difficult thing to avoid; no amount of "keeping your eyes on the road" will keep you pure of heart and mind. Lust is impossible to completely defeat this side of heaven. Jesus ups the demand of the law from "thou shalt not commit adultery" to "thou shalt not think about it" to force men to come face to face with their failure. Jesus doesn't have coping strategies to suggest; instead, he is mighty to save those who cannot cope.

THE HAPPINESS PARADOX

Do you think that it's a coincidence that clowns are assumed—in nearly every single instance—to be depressed and/or scary? They're anything but the happy that they appear to be on the surface, right? We assume that anyone who would apply a garish grease-paint smile to their face must be crying on the inside. I suspect that we think this because there's a paradox at work—whether we acknowledge it or not—in our lives: the harder we try to be happy, the further we seem to get from our goal.

The 2015 Pixar film *Inside Out* got at this idea with a story that involved the internal emotions of a young girl. The emotions, anthropomorphized by Amy Poehler (Joy), Phyllis Smith (Sadness), Bill Hader (Fear), Lewis Black (Anger), and Mindy Kaling (Disgust), try to figure out how to keep their little girl happy. It seems obvious, at first, that job number one is to keep Sadness at bay, and let Joy be in charge. As it turns out, though—in a brilliant and true insight by the film—sadness is an integral part of a well-rounded emotional life. This is, for most people, hard to accept.

The New York Times published an article in 2013 by Oliver Burkeman called "Who Goes to Work to Have Fun?" in which Burkeman sheds light on this happiness paradox. He's discussing office environments that do all they can to keep their employees "happy" but are getting mixed results. Here's part of what he says:

> The problem here is an organizational version of the "paradox of hedonism," best expressed by John Stuart Mill: "Ask yourself whether you are happy, and you cease to be so." The attempt to impose happiness

is self-sabotaging. Psychologists have shown that positive-thinking affirmations make people with low self-esteem feel worse; that patients with panic disorders can become more anxious when they try to relax; and that an ability to experience negative emotions, rather than struggling to exclude them, is crucial for mental health.[3]

As it turns out, happiness is not just a difficult thing to achieve; it's impossible. I don't mean that no one can ever be happy; that's definitely not true. I mean that, apparently, no one can be happy *by deciding to be happy*. Play Bobby McFerrin's "Don't Worry Be Happy" to someone who is truly sad and find out how far that gets you.

But the paradoxes don't end with our apparent inability to produce happiness in ourselves. The real mystery is that, despite ample evidence to the contrary, most people remain convinced that they *can,* and do, choose to be happy.

CHOOSING TO BE HAPPY

Here's a strange confession: the arc of my ministerial career changed in a bathroom. Luckily, however, it wasn't for any reason that you might expect, given just that information. It was, in fact, much less salacious. I was visiting a friend whose mother had recently passed away after a long, arduous battle with cancer; we were both staying at his recently-widowed father's house. I happened to be in the bathroom one morning, and there, sitting on the table next to the commode, was a stack of *Watchtower* magazines. The one on top featured a well-known mega-church pastor's smiling face and a headline promising a number of suggested resolutions for a blessed new year. Flipping into the magazine, I came across the list, and one of them immediately jumped out at me: choose to be happy. Intrigued,

I read the accompanying paragraph.

The pastor described a time when a car wash had scratched his Lexus. When the car came out of the wash and was presented to him, he said that he could have chosen to be angry about it. After all, his car was scratched. But, he explained, he instead decided to be happy. He then described the significant personal and spiritual benefits that can be achieved by choosing to be happy.

I was floored. Flabbergasted. There I was, sitting in the home of a man who had recently lost the love of his life to a terrible disease, and this pastor was counseling him (admittedly, not directly, but still...) to "choose" to be happy. After all, didn't he do it when his Lexus got scratched? I happened to mention how much this advice galled me to my friend, and suggested that it was much more pastoral to avoid minimizing someone's pain by suggesting that they had the ability to simply "choose to be happy." My friend then encouraged me to share the sentiment with his father, the bereaved, assuming it would make him feel better. Reluctantly, I did. His response surprised me even more than the article.

"I just don't think you can choose to be happy," I remember saying; "I think you can choose to *act* happy, but actually *being* happy is something else entirely, and it's insulting to someone who's truly grieving to imply that they should be able to be happy." The response was an angry one: "What do you think I've been doing for the past six months?" I couldn't believe it. Here was a man who was demonstrably and inarguably unhappy. He was rightfully grieving the loss of his wife and trying to prepare himself for a life without her. I felt as though I was on his side of things, giving him permission to be unhappy, but he saw my comment as a judgment: I was calling him a faker. He wanted the world to see him as fine, and I was suggesting that he wasn't. How dare I?

My sin was calling the supposedly possible ("be happy") impossible. But, as much as it hurt my friend's father's feelings, lived experience bears it out: it is impossible to choose to be happy. It is only possible to choose to *act* happy. After all, if it was possible to choose happiness, wouldn't we all do so, all the time? True, some psychologists have suggested that "acting" happy can produce actual happiness, but even that—if it's even true—takes a lot of work, and starts with much intentional mask-wearing…it's not merely a choice. My friend's father was unhappy…and he had good reason to be. Healing comes when we can acknowledge our pain, admit that we can't just choose to be better all by ourselves, and call out for a savior: one who has promised to come, not to the healthy, but to the sick (Mark 2:17).

IMPOSSIBLE ATHLETICS

Bode Miller was the clear goat (not G.O.A.T. as in "greatest of all time"—the other, negative one) of the 2006 Torino Winter Olympics. America's best skier, Miller came into the Olympics expected to medal in all five events that he entered. He became infamous in the days leading up to the competition by making repeated claims that he didn't care if he won, that he just wanted to have a good time, and by admitting that he had often skied drunk. Having won two medals four years earlier in Salt Lake City, Miller was the "darling black sheep" of American skiing. Coming into Torino, though, he was outspokenly apathetic: "Whether somebody wants me to get five gold medals or whatever it is, I sort of feel like they are all other people's concerns and issues, not really mine…I don't really care what everybody else says."

For those Olympic fans out there, you know what happened. He won zero medals, and took major heat for saying the same thing after the Olympics (basically, to paraphrase, "I don't care") that he'd said before them. Pilloried for four years, Miller was dismissed in the run-up to the 2010 Games. Called "a clown" by much of the sports media; he was completely overshadowed by Lindsey Vonn coming into those Vancouver Games. In fact, he quit the U.S. ski team shortly after Torino, training only when he wanted.

Less than a year before Vancouver, though, Miller discovered in himself the desire to ski for his country. He applied for reinstatement and was granted it. (I'm sure it didn't hurt that he remained one of the best skiers in any downhill discipline in the world). In an Olympics in which all attention was focused on Vonn and he was all but forgotten, all Miller did was rack up three medals (a gold, silver, and bronze) in five events.

Miller credited the medal count to his attitude. It is interesting to note that his attitude was the same in Vancouver as it was in Torino. It's the exterior forces that had changed. Here's an excerpt from an article published shortly after the Vancouver Olympics.[4]

> As for the Olympics, he added, it's not about obsessing over medals—and certainly not about obsessing over other people obsessing about your winning medals.
>
> Today, as he occupies the pinnacle of his sport on its biggest stage, having cemented his stature as the greatest American skier ever, he says that it's about "having fun, about skiing like I did when I was a kid."
>
> As a teenager, Miller showed the sky's-the-limit-potential he first delivered on with a pair of silvers in Salt Lake City eight years ago. But that success may have actually hurt him, setting him up for the huge fall of 2006, when other people's expecta-

tions made him surly and, worse, almost defiantly non-competitive.

And there you have it: Pressure from the outside "made him surly and...defiantly non-competitive." It was only when he was forgotten about, when the pressure was released, when he was branded a clown, that his performance reached his potential. I don't think it's too much of a stretch to say that Miller's performance was freed when he was seen for what he was: an over-hyped clown. Miller could, in Vancouver, own his clownish nature and ski without feeling the impossible-to-live-up-to pressure to be the cold-blooded Olympic assassin we all wanted him to be, but which he never was.

Miller's story serves as a highlighter on our repeating message of possible and impossible, judgment and love, critique and grace, pressure and release. It is when pressure is released, when the law is lifted, and when the impossible is acknowledged, that "performance" can meet expectation.

EVERYDAY LIFE

In this chapter, I've shared a few examples from day-to-day life that show how pervasive the impossible is. In my experience, the more honest we can be about this facet of our lives, the truer the lives we live will actually be. I understand, though, that it can be hard to accept. It's going to get worse before it gets better. Before we get to why the impossibility of life is actually Good News, we have to consider one more impossible thing: your freedom.

CHAPTER 6

IMPOSSIBLE FREEDOM

Our ability to convince ourselves that things are difficult and not impossible hinges on the fact that we have already convinced ourselves of something else that isn't true: that we are free agents, possessors of unbound wills, walking out into the world every day making unfettered choices as we see fit.

Now, I understand that this is dangerous ground. From William Wallace to Patrick Henry, our freedom is probably our most closely guarded possession. Any challenge to it, or any suggestion that it isn't quite as complete as we assume it is, and the claws come out. That's what I'm aiming to do, though, in this chapter: challenge your freedom. But listen, I'm not going to suggest that you're some kind of automaton, or robot, a soul watching helplessly through the eyes of a body that you can't control. I'm just going to suggest that you're less "in control" than you assume that you are. And further, I'll show you why it's actually *good* news, not bad, that you are less free than you think.

Truthfully, the suggestion that your will isn't actually all that free doesn't have to be a scary one. All it implies is that the choices you make every day, from what to say to what to eat to what to wear, aren't as free as you think they are. In fact, they're bound—in other words, tied up. They have metaphorical ropes wrapped around them, every rope leading to some other non-you force that's pulling your will in a certain direction. Most of our choices have several (if not dozens) of these ropes tied around them, all being yanked.

There's a wonderful *Key & Peele* sketch in which the two actors are on the phone with their wives and change their vocal attitudes—from effete patron of the arts to boisterous gangsta rapper—depending on the passersby who are within earshot. They alter their personas depending on who's around. Who can't identify with that? One force pulls you one way, another force pulls you another. Think of yourself as the central point in a giant, multi-directional game of tug-o-war. And yet, we spend all of our time loudly asserting our freedom. True freedom, it turns out, comes from recognizing the ropes and calling out for help, not from denying that the ropes are there.

EVEN A NECKTIE ISN'T FREE

There's a scene in the 2011 film *The Adjustment Bureau* in which Matt Damon, playing a young, on-the-rise politician, gives a speech to his supporters. He talks about how people call him "authentic," which the audience rousingly applauds. He quickly quiets the crowd, though, with, "But here's the problem. This isn't even my tie." And then he gives one of the most eloquent descriptions of the bound will that you'll ever see in a Hollywood movie. Here's what he says:

> This tie was selected for me by a group of specialists in Tenafly, New Jersey, who chose it over 56 other ties we tested. In fact, our data suggests that I have to stick to either a tie that is red or a tie that is blue. A yellow tie made it look as if I was taking my situation lightly...a silver tie meant that I'd forgotten

my roots. My shoes...you know, shiny shoes we associate with high-priced lawyers and bankers. If you want to get a working man's vote you've got to scuff up your shoes a little bit, but you can't scuff them up so much that you alienate the lawyers and the bankers because you need them to pay for the specialists back in Tenafly. So what is the proper scuffing amount? Do you know that we actually paid a consultant...to tell us that this is the perfect amount of scuffing.

Incredible, right? It's unlikely that you are a politician who hires a consultant to advise you on your wardrobe, but you are no less bound by those forces pulling at you than Matt Damon's character is. Think about all the factors—"forces"—that you take into account when you get dressed in the morning. Aren't we all bound by the sort of forces he mentions in his speech?

We want to be perceived in a certain way, and so dress accordingly. Even those among us (hippies, punks, Goths, etc.) who claim to be rebelling against "society's rules" find themselves constrained to think, act, and dress a certain way. There's a reason that the Goth is as easily picked out of a crowd as the hedge fund manager. The evidence of our lives suggests that our wills are bound even in things as pedestrian as what we wear out of the house. We imagine that our choices of clothing, coffee, and career are free. How often have you agonized over the wording of an email, perhaps to a boss, or to someone else you're trying to impress (or appease)? Someone might argue that you're "free" to type whatever you want. It sure doesn't feel like freedom to the person sitting at the keyboard, though. Just think about all the sources (parents, society, friends, goals, etc.) of pressure that tug you one way or another. Suddenly, our "freedom" begins to reveal itself as an illusion, and the realization that our wills are bound by all sorts of forces becomes more and more obvious.

SATAN IS (AND ISN'T) YOUR MOTOR

> My intentions are good, and earnest, and true
> But under my hood is internal combustion power
> And Satan is my motor

Cake's song "Satan Is My Motor," from the 1998 album *Prolonging the Magic*, is also a wonderful description of the human predicament: we know what we want, but it doesn't always work out that we get it. We aren't as free to "do what we want" as we might think that we are. Cake's Joel McCrea uses a car to illustrate his point; he's got everything in place but he can't control what's under the hood. Here's the first verse of the song:

> I've got wheels of polished steel
> I've got tires that grab the road
> I've got seats that selflessly hold my friends
> And a trunk that can carry the heaviest of loads
> I've got a mind that can steer me to your house
> And a heart that can bring you red flowers
> My intentions are good, and earnest, and true
> But under my hood is internal combustion power
> And Satan is my motor

It's an apt illustration: he can manage all the superficial details about his car, but the thing that actually makes the operation go—the motor—is too much for him to control. It drives the car wherever it wants. It doesn't matter that his wheels are shined and that he's got new tires; it doesn't even matter that his heart and his mind are in the right places. The motor is in charge, and when he looks at the results of his life, he can only come to one conclusion: Satan is his motor.

I can't listen to this song without thinking of Paul's words in Romans 7: "I do not understand my own actions. For I do not do what I want, but I do the very thing I hate. Now if I do what I do not want, I agree with the law, that it is good. So now it is no longer I who do it, but sin that dwells within me. For I know that nothing good dwells in me, that is, in my flesh. For I have the desire to do what is right, but not the ability to carry it out. For I do not do the good I want, but the evil I do not want is what I keep on doing" (vv. 15-19).

This disconnect between what we want to do and what we actually find ourselves doing points to a fundamental—and practical—truth about life and Christianity's influence on it: your problem isn't on the surface. It's under the hood.

On one occasion several years ago, my car died. I called up my insurance company because I'm completely hopeless when it comes to cars—as I am with most things. The claims adjuster on the line called up a list of approved mechanics in my area and recommended one to which I could arrange to have the car towed. When I arrived at the recommended shop, though, I realized that this was going to be a fool's errand: it was a body shop, not a full-service mechanic's. In other words, if I had a dented quarter-panel (a term I learned from *Days of Thunder*), they could help me. If I wanted to install suicide doors, this was the place. Unfortunately, I was having engine trouble, and they couldn't help me.

In our Christian lives, we are quick to take ourselves to the body shop. We think we just need some of the dents smoothed out. We need to learn a little bit more about being a good father. We need some help with a Bible-reading plan. We need to stay more faithful in the face of adversity. We need instruction about managing our finances like a disciple of Christ.

We do everything we can to ignore the truth: we need a new motor.

Martin Luther suggested that everyone is a horse, ridden either by Christ or by Satan. The horse doesn't get to choose. Cake is on to this same idea. We choose our wheels, our seats, and the trunk. We can make everything on the outside look perfect. We can make sure that we're set up to succeed. We don't get to choose what's under the hood. And unfortunately, it's what's under the hood that wields the most power.

This bad news—that all our superficial work is useless—is totally overcome by the good news that Christ has unseated Satan as the rider of our horse. He has removed Satan as the engine of our car and gotten under the hood himself: "Therefore, if anyone is in Christ, he is a new creation. The old has passed away; behold, the new has come" (2 Corinthians 5:17). He did this by becoming sin, even though he knew no sin, so that we might become the righteousness of God (2 Corinthians 5:21).

"Satan Is My Motor" still describes our human experience, just like Romans 7 does. But it does not describe the actual truth of our situation. Satan is no longer our motor. Paul exults in Christ Jesus who has delivered him from "this body of death" that he has described in Romans 7. We are no longer driving in sin...though it sure feels that way. That feeling is merely the echo of an old truth, the stink of an old motor. Our sin went to the cross with Christ, who has now given us his goodness, earnestness, and truth. In him, we have become the righteousness of God. Jesus is your motor.

GETTING AWAY FROM IT ALL

The 2012 Paul Rudd/Jennifer Aniston film *Wanderlust* is a very underrated comedy. Directed by David Wain, *Wanderlust* is the story of a "normal" couple (Rudd and Aniston) who lose their jobs and home and find themselves spending time at a hippie commune called "Elysium" in Georgia.

It's a classic fish-out-of-water story, with Rudd and Aniston as the buttoned-up squares trying to fit in to a community in which everything is shared equally and freely. Elysium has even gone so far as to remove the door from the communal bathroom. Despite the intentions of the community (live together in perfect harmony), there are downsides. There are small instances of unpleasantness (Joe Lo Truglio plays a character never seen in a stitch of clothing), but things really go wrong when Paul Rudd swats a fly. What happens next is a hilarious illustration of our inability to get away from the rules and pressures of life—those forces pulling at us—even in a theoretical utopia like Elysium.

When he's accused of "killing a defenseless animal," Paul Rudd protests that he "just" swatted a fly. After several more rounds of chastisement, he apologizes, saying that he's "just trying to learn all the rules." Seth, the commune's pseudo-yogi spiritual leader, immediately pipes up: "There are no rules here." "Except 'no swatting flies,'" protests Rudd. "That's not a rule," retorts Seth, "it's just a way of thinking about stuff."

So there are rules. Rules, as you have likely found in your own life, are inescapable. No one actually wants to live under the Outback Steakhouse's dictum "No Rules, Just Right." Without rules, we know, life doesn't work very well. We can't all just do whatever we want to do all the time. Rules, we imagine, are how we can keep other people in line. They're how we get other people to come around to our "ways of thinking about stuff."

One of the best jokes in *Wanderlust* is that the hippies have been in rebellion for so long, the things they're rebelling against (for instance, Walkmen and fax machines) are all hilariously out-of-date. The residents of Elysium reveal a truth about human nature: in our desire to proclaim our freedom, we rebel against whoever we've decided are the legalists in our lives. But we can't get out of our own way. We need to make sure that our rebellious brothers and sisters agree with us…and pretty soon, we find ourselves to be no different from those legalists we hate so much.

The truth about human beings is that we are addicted to law, to rule-making, and so even when we rebel against the rule-making of others, we tend to set up rules to govern our rebellion. This is true even in the most judgment-free environments in America, including the annual Burning Man festival in the ad-hoc town of Black Rock City, Nevada. Several years ago, the now-defunct ESPN website Grantland sent its Rembert Browne to report on the event, and he came back with what we might think of as the predictable report: it's a crazy, free-wheeling, no-rules-just-right time out there on "deep playa." Here's what passes for a thesis of his article:

> Speaking of family, as I split up from the bike gang to go explore on my own, I randomly ran into a friend from grade school who I then proceeded to dance with for two hours. After that, I spoke with a father who gave us his philosophy on bringing his kids to Black Rock City. In less than 10 minutes, he convinced me that this place, often characterized as a dust-soaked den of sex and drugs, was a wonderful space for kids. Between the programming and activities and the exposure to a judgment-free environment so early on, there was no better place for youth. While he was telling me this, his son was passing out peanut M&Ms to passersby and waving a stick of incense. I think Pops was right.[6]

It should be noted that "dust-soaked den of sex and drugs" would be a pretty broadly agreed-upon description of Black Rock City, a town that only exists for the week during Burning Man. The question is not whether Black Rock City is such a den (it surely is), but whether or not it is actually the escape that it purports to be.

Browne asserts that Burning Man is "a judgment-free environment." Does Burning Man succeed in a way that *Wanderlust*'s Elysium cannot? If so, sign me up! I'll bail on "the default world" (as Burners call the world outside of Black Rock City). But check out a couple of other quotes from Browne's piece:

- "Moving cars are frowned upon once they've been parked."

- "It all started with my revelation to them that this was my first time. I'd noticed that if you're chill and appear to be present for the right reasons, people love first-timers."

- "So Diplo was in town. I heard rumors that he was going to play a show, but didn't want to be that new guy who seemed more interested in a famous DJ doing a set than the spirit of Burning Man. So I relayed the message to just a few people. But, secretly, I wanted to see it so bad."

- "Also, we went to go get some ice. This was notable because we had to use cash. See, there's no money in Black Rock City. The only economy is the gift economy—not barter, gifting. That is, except for ice. It wasn't surprising that ice would be the one example of capitalism to sneak into Black Rock City, because it was by far the most precious, sought-after commodity."

- "I finally went to sleep around 5:45 a.m. I felt as if I were finally a part of the fabric of my camp. I'd gained the respect of the longtime campers. Even in this semi-utopian city, earning respect still mattered."

So Burning Man is a lot more like the outside world than Burners would ever admit, isn't it? There are plenty of rules; they're just not written down (like the "no swatting flies" rule in Elysium. In fact, it's easy to imagine a Burner suggesting that these are "just ways of thinking about stuff."). The unwritten rules are enforced as vigorously (and perhaps more so) than the written ones. Look back through Browne's quotes. If they sound familiar, it's because you know the exact same thing to be true in your subdivision, your schoolyard, your office, and your in-laws' house.

In truth, Burning Man is exactly like the default world. It *is* the default world. It cannot be anything else. God has put his Law into our minds and written it on our hearts (Hebrews 8:10): we carry it wherever we go. And if God's Law is there, its pale human shadow is there too: be how you're expected to be, go along, fit in, earn respect.

Does Burning Man or Elysium sound great to you? Or do they sound like they'd make you tear your hair out in frustration? Either way, the lesson is the same: you are just as bound to the rules as the people against whom you're rebelling...and you're just as in need of a savior. Whether you work hard to follow the rules or work hard to break them, you are bound by them. Every single one of us is bound by the agreed-upon ropes of the communities in which we place (or find) ourselves. Neither Elysium nor Burning Man, apparently, is savior enough, despite the claims of their residents. In the end, the Burners and the Squares are all the same, subject to the rules, wherever they come from. This fact makes the Good News all the more wonderful: that Jesus died for everyone's sins, no matter what kind of commune (or gated community) you live in.

THE DAY SPA OF DEATH

Martin Luther wrote that the quest for glory could never be satisfied. Instead, he claimed, it had to be extinguished. In other words, it's impossible to actually reach the point at which you're satisfied with the point you've reached. The carrot is always just beyond our grasp. John D. Rockefeller was nodding to this idea, saying, when allegedly asked how much money would be enough for him, "just a little bit more." There are a thousand personal-to-you examples of this. As soon as you get the promotion you've been pining for, you realize that there are several more levels of management to attain. Hugh Hefner must always move on to the next younger, sexier woman. In the 2016 film *The Founder*, Ray Kroc (of McDonald's fame) is asked, "When is enough going to be enough for you?" His answer: "Honestly? Probably never."

Frasier (in a season 10 episode called "Door Jam") again provides a perfect illustration here: After an amazing afternoon of coddling in an exclusive day spa, Frasier and Niles say, "I feel like I've been rubbed by angels" and "I've never felt better in my life." But then they notice a golden door, through which they are forbidden to go. "It's for our gold-level members only," they are told. Immediately, the wonder of the day turns to hatred. "Just how are we supposed to enjoy *this*?" wonders Frasier angrily, gesturing around at the same spa about which he'd just been raving. When asked later what the place was like, he spits, "It was a hell hole!"

After trying everything to wrangle an invitation through the golden door, Frasier and Niles are having coffee with their friend Roz (Peri Gilpin), who chides them: "You only want to go in there because you can't. How much better can it be? And then, what if you do get in the gold door? What's next, the diamond door? And after that a titanium door? And after that a plutonium door?" Roz knows her Luther: there is no end to the human struggle, the human quest for achievement. There will forever be another door through which we feel we must pass.

Of course, it turns out that Roz actually knows someone with enough influence to get Frasier and Niles through the gold door, and it turns out that she's wrong. The gold-level spa is infinitely better than the silver-level spa. Frasier describes the "relaxation grotto" in the gold level as "paradise." But it turns out that there is a platinum door! When Niles wants to go through the unguarded door, Frasier cries, "This is heaven! Right here and now! Why do we have to think about someplace else!" Niles retorts, "This is only heaven for people who can't get in to the real heaven…the platinum heaven!" Finally, Frasier wonders, "Why can't we be happy?"

When Frasier goes over to the platinum door, to take a peek through it, an employee of the spa tells him, "You're not allowed through there…please remain in the relaxation grotto." With that, the relaxation grotto becomes an intolerable prison: "Please remain in the relaxation grotto?" moans Frasier. "Have crueler words ever been spoken?"

So finally, Frasier and Niles go through the platinum door, and the truth is revealed to them: there is no platinum-level spa. They are outside, with the dumpsters and garbage, locked out of the spa altogether. The Crane boys' quest for glory was extinguished. They couldn't *not* go through that final door; they couldn't be satisfied with the beauty of the relaxation grotto they were already enjoying. Thankfully for Christians, we are never alone when we find ourselves out with the garbage, for it is there that Christ finds us.

YOUR LAWN IS A MESS (AND SO ARE YOU)

You've heard that there are two types of people in the world: Beatles people and Elvis people. Or creamy peanut butter people and crunchy peanut butter people. Allow me to suggest that there are two *other* kinds of people in the world: people who are good at hiding their messiness and people whose messiness is visible to everyone. The people who are good at hiding their messiness often run large and complicated businesses like hedge funds, or hospitals, or multi-national corporations. They have good haircuts and bespoke clothing. Sometimes you'll see on the Internet that the messiness of one of these people has come out, and everyone is shocked.

When I think about these two types of people, I think about South Florida lawns. This might seem strange to you, but if you've lived in South Florida, as I have, you'll know that almost every single homeowner pays a lawn service to care for their grass, shrubberies, and trees. South Florida flora is some of the hardiest stuff in the world; it's like you need a green thumb black belt (green thumb belt?) to tame the stuff. The result of lawn care being universally hired out is that every lawn is immaculately kept. Not a blade of grass is out of place. But there's always that one house.

Again, you know the one I mean: the house that you'd be sure was abandoned (or inhabited only by ghosts) if you didn't see the cars coming and going. The kids don't play in the yard, but that's because they'd probably be devoured by the alligators sure to be living in there.

There was one such house in my neighborhood during the time I spent in Florida. For a time, in fact, my neighbors were concerned that my own yard would turn into a sort-of "Everglades East," but they sent an envoy to guilt us into paying someone to, at least occasionally, beat back Mother Nature. One day I drove past this other house—which I appreciated because it made my yard look good—and noticed a sign out front. The sign said:

> Native plants bring life to this landscape. This "Florida Friendly" property is a model landscape that conserves and protects our precious water resources and provides valuable wildlife habitat. It has been certified by Broward County as an official NatureScape property.

Now look. I value protecting wildlife habitat and precious water resources as much as anyone. But if I'm honest, my first thought upon reading that sign was more self-centered: "What a great scam!" I thought. "I've got to get one of those signs so that I can be totally lazy about my lawn!" I was envisioning a sign that, no matter what it actually said, conveyed the following message: "It's not gross, we swear. It's supposed to be this way!"

So let me be more specific about the two kinds of people in the world. There are two kinds: those who cover up their mess and those who justify their mess. It's the difference between the advertising executive who gets a haircut once a week to announce to the world, "I'm not a mess! Look at my perfect hair!" and the guy on your college campus with the bongo drums who hasn't washed his hair in six months to announce to the world, "I'm not a mess! I'm countercultural!"

Jesus calls us to make a different announcement to the world: "I'm a mess!" Neither the advertising executive nor the bongo drummer has it all together, but denial isn't going to save the executive from his prescription addiction and psychiatrist's bills or the bongo drummer from joblessness and homelessness.

When Peter first comes into contact with Jesus he says, "Depart from me, for I am a sinful man" (Luke 5:8). In other words, "I'm a mess!" But later, when everyone is abandoning Jesus, Peter knows that there's nowhere else a mess like him can go. "To whom shall we go?" he says. "You have the words of eternal life" (John 6:68).

You and I are both a mess. There's just no getting around it. Maybe our yards show it, and maybe they don't. Maybe our hair shows it, and maybe it doesn't. It's true all the same. We are not free to not be messes. But instead of hiding our messes or trying to pretend that we "like it this way," we can cast our hope on the one who came into the world to clean up our messes, to put himself in our place, and to save our lives.

THE LOSE-LOSE OF LETTER JACKETS

Anyone who played sports in high school knows about letter jackets. It was the thing you always wanted to get, and the thing you wore at every opportunity. My relationship with my own letter jacket was a complicated one: I was awarded a letter during my sophomore year...for marching band. As if that wasn't indignity enough, the marching band letter was a totally different style than the sports letters, making it impossible for me to pretend that I was a "real" letterman. Eventually, though, I was awarded several athletic letters and could wear my letter jacket proudly. I never got to let a girl wear it, but you can't have everything.

But what happens to a letter jacket after graduation? Where do letter jackets go when they retire? Do they go to a farm upstate? Perhaps, but the one place they definitely do not go is into a freshman dorm room closet. I've literally never seen anyone wear a high school letter jacket when they are no longer in high school. Nothing would seem more desperate or pathetic: clutching at bygone greatness. In a scene from the first season of the television show *Community*, Troy (Donald Glover) tries to make a decision about his letter jacket, because people at the community college that he now attends have been making fun of him for wearing it. Troy says, "People have been clowning me about this jacket since I got here, but if I take it off to make them happy, that just makes me weak, right?" His new friend Jeff (Joel McHale) turns to him and says, "Listen: it doesn't matter. You lose the jacket to please them, you keep it to piss them off. Either way, it's for them. That's what's weak."

Now, it may be obvious to all of us that Troy's mistake was wearing his letter jacket to college in the first place. That's not what I'm interested in. What interests me is the theological insight of his new friend: whether he takes the jacket off or keeps it on, he's doing it "for them." That's what's weak.

This is a perfect illustration of the inescapability of pressure and the bound nature of our wills. Whether we struggle to obey the rules or we reject them, we are under their power. Think of how you related to your parents when you first left home: did you resolve to be just like them…or did you resolve to be nothing like them? As Troy's friend Jeff would say, it doesn't matter. Either way, they are still the ones influencing you. If we strive to mold ourselves into today's Barbie-doll aesthetic or go the other way into shabby-chic, Barbie is still directing our decisions. "Do not be deceived," St. Paul writes to the Galatians, "God is not mocked" (6:7). Another way to say what Paul is saying here is, don't fall into the trap of thinking that the rules can't touch you. You can obey or you can rebel, but the rules still control you. There is no escape.

NO FREEDOM IN LOVE

Remember *The Adjustment Bureau* and its desperate claim that our wills can be free, despite featuring an incredible scene that seems to argue the exact opposite? The final nail in *The Adjustment Bureau*'s coffin is an ironic one. It is his love for Emily Blunt that compels Matt Damon to continue bucking the Bureau and attempting to make his own way. The Bureau keeps trying to bump him back on plan, and the reason he's so resistant is that he wants to be with the woman with whom he's fallen in love. But here's the irony: he hasn't made a rational free will decision to desire Blunt! Of course he hasn't! No one makes a rational decision about love. We call it "falling" in love for a reason! It happens to us; it's not chosen by us. We might say it "binds" us. It's another thing that throws a rope around us and starts pulling. And thank goodness it does: our track record of rational decision-making isn't great. The truth is scary and comforting at the same time: our wills are more bound than we thought they were, which means that more is impossible for us than we thought. If we were on our own, that would be terrible news indeed.

True bondage, it turns out, is the result of our dogged insistence that we are free. True freedom, conversely, comes from acknowledging our bondage and calling out for Jesus, the one who came to set the captives free (Luke 4:18).

CHAPTER 7

FROM IMPOSSIBLE TO DIFFICULT

I remember once riding in a car with a friend and discussing Jesus' Sermon on the Mount. You know, like you do. We were talking about how audacious Jesus' claims were, that lust was morally equivalent to adultery, that anger was equivalent to murder, et cetera. This friend of mine eventually said that he just didn't believe that that was true. I wondered if he was saying that he didn't believe Jesus really said those things, or if he believed that Jesus was wrong in his assertions. His answer was really neither: "I believe he really said that," said my friend, "but I don't believe he really meant it."

Many of us harbor this feeling deep in our subconscious. Jesus just said so many hard things, right? I mean, he said that in order to be his follower you have to hate your father and your mother (Luke 14:26); he said that you cannot even so much as think someone a fool (Matthew 5:22)…and so on.

We're susceptible to the same logical error that Christopher Hitchens and Jacques del Conte made (discussed in Chapter 2), that wise lawmakers don't make laws that are impossible to follow. Therefore, we assume that Jesus, as he was saying these impossible-sounding things, really must have meant something a little less stringent. So when we're presented with a seemingly impossible requirement, our first urge is to think to ourselves, "Well, he couldn't really have meant *that*. He must have meant this other (not impossible, but merely difficult) thing." He doesn't, though. He means the impossible.

THE SEEDS OR THE SOWER

Consider the parable of the sower, which is an absolutely classic example of an impossible story misinterpreted into difficult marching orders. You know the story (it's in Matthew 13): there's a sower sowing seeds, and seeds fall on different kinds of soil. Some fall on the path, some on rocky ground, some among thorns. All of these seeds fail to flourish. They're eaten by birds, can't be sustained by insufficient soil, or are choked by the thorns. Only seeds that fall on good soil flourish. The seeds that are eaten by birds symbolize people who don't understand the word of the kingdom. The seeds sown on rocky ground symbolize people who fall away due to trouble or persecution because of a lack of deep roots of faith. The seed sown amongst the thorns symbolize people whose faith is choked away by the cares of the world. Only the seed sown on the good soil, representing people who hear the word and understand it, can take root and grow, bearing fruit, thirty-, sixty-, or even a hundred-fold.

Most people, Christians included, approach this passage having already come to the conclusion that they are going to have to save themselves, and that self-salvation will be difficult. Why this presupposition? The problem is that we are inveterate *doers*, not able to trust others to do things for us. We like, when we see a problem, to roll up our sleeves and get to work. We are *producers*; we like tangible results. We like to look back at the end of a day and see a job well done. But truly introspective people—people who are honest with themselves about them-selves—know that things don't work out so simply. Things aren't right just the way they are. People feel the friction between the way things are and the way they're supposed to be. That's why everyone's striving, working, struggling. Every person you see on the street—every person you meet in your life—is trying to figure out a way to get from the way things are to the way things ought to be. Because at the end of most days, we look back and don't see a job well done. Our tangible results are disappointing. Our personal production department hasn't met its quota. We got to work, but our work left us short of our goal. Exhaustingly, we wake up the next morning, get to work again, and more often than not come away once again defeated. In this way, life can be tremendously sad.

It seems to me that, in general, most people can agree about that diagnosis: life is tremendously sad. We struggle daily to be the people we want to be and realize that we're still—in the main—the people we've always been. The question that must then be asked is: what's the prescription? What will rescue us from this body of death (Romans 7:24)? What's the medicine we can take to fix things? How do we heal ourselves from this sickness? Like I said, we are workers. We're producers. We want to get to work healing ourselves, but what do we do? What's the rehab regimen? Christians often, in their search for self-heal-ing, turn to verses like these from Romans 8, or the many like them in the New Testament: "For those who live according to the flesh set their minds on the things of the flesh, but those who live according to the Spirit set their minds on the things of the Spirit. To set the mind on the flesh is death, but to set the mind on the Spirit is life and peace" (vv. 5-6). There you go, it seems…a neat prescription: set your mind on the things of the Spirit, and you will have life and peace. And don't live according to the flesh, because that leads to death. Sounds simple

enough, right? And to our workaholic ears—our ears addicted
to doing things, to production—it sounds downright attrac-
tive. It sounds like good medicine. But I think St. Paul is saying
something a bit different. And here we can turn back to the
parable of the sower for interpretive help.

Our natural instinct as human beings is to interpret that
parable in the same way that we wanted to interpret those sentences from Romans 8. There, it was "live according to the
Spirit, don't live according to the flesh." Here, it's "make sure
you are the seed sown on good soil. Don't be like the seed sown
on the path, or on rocky ground, or among the thorns."

Here's the thing, though. Jesus has told the parable of the
sower in such a way that we simply cannot interpret it like that!
That natural human interpretation—be careful what kind of
seed you are—makes literally no sense in the context of the
parable. How can a seed choose which kind of soil in which to
be sown? It's impossible! It's *the sower* who sows the seeds! The
seeds mindlessly fall wherever they are sown. Jesus has given us
the most passive illustration possible. We are not the sower in
his story. We are the seeds.

Now, this is disturbing. I understand that. It seems to take
away our agency. If we're just the seeds, and we're powerless
to control where the sower sows us, how can we control our
fates? How can we heal ourselves? How can we make sure we're
those flourishing seeds? Well, we can't. Spoiler alert: we don't
control our fates! Remember *The Adjustment Bureau*. But take
comfort, this is Good News: the fact that we are passive seeds
being sown by an active sower is only scary until we know that
the sower is God almighty, Father of Jesus Christ, savior and
redeemer of the world. To people who can't always—or, let's be
honest, ever—control where our minds are set, hearing "to set
the mind on the flesh is death, but to set the mind on the Spirit
is life and peace" is terrifyingly scary, until you read what Paul

writes directly before and after it. There are words of immense comfort in Romans 8:9: "But you are not in the flesh; you are in the Spirit, since the Spirit of God dwells in you" (NRSV).

Notice what's missing? There are no conditions! No, "if/then" statements. Just a pronouncement: "You are not in the flesh!" And guess what? If you look back at the scary verses—"to set the mind on the flesh is death, but to set the mind on the Spirit is life and peace"—there are no conditions there either! No if/then. These verses are not prescriptions for you to use to heal yourself; they are descriptions of the goodness of the Good News!

"To set the mind on the Spirit is life and peace." This is the sweetest Gospel, beautiful music to the ears of us who worry that we don't adequately set our minds on the Spirit, that we might have been sown on the path, or on rocky soil, or among the thorns, we whose hard work doesn't yield the results we'd hoped and whose production departments have fallen well short of expectation. Right after we realize our shortcomings, our inability to do what we want, and our compulsion to do the things we hate, when we call out to God for a savior, we get one. "Thanks be to God through Jesus Christ our Lord" (Romans 7:25).

Paul's not done with the Good News, either: "There is therefore now no condemnation for those who are in Christ Jesus. For the law of the Spirit of life has set you free in Christ Jesus from the law of sin and death. For God has done what the law, weakened by the flesh, could not do. By sending his own Son in the likeness of sinful flesh and for sin, he condemned sin in the flesh, in order that the righteous requirement of the law might be fulfilled in us, who walk not according to the flesh but according to the Spirit" (Romans 8:1-4).

Hear the Good News right now: On account of Christ, you don't have to worry about whether you are in the Spirit or in the flesh. God has acted. On account of Christ, the God who gave his life for you, you are in the Spirit. You don't have to worry about the kind of soil in which you're planted. God has acted. On account of Christ, you are the seed thrown on good soil!

We agreed on the diagnosis: simply put, life is impossible. What's the prescription? How do you heal yourself? You don't. You are healed. There is no condemnation for those in Christ Jesus, and there is nothing more you must do. We don't need to be doers anymore. We've been promoted! We're not in the production department. We're in the celebration department.

So let's celebrate. Let's bask in the sunshine of a day in which there is no work to be done, our tangible results are prepared for us in advance by Christ, and the doors of our personal production departments are locked tight and there are banners hanging out the windows that read, "It is Finished." Production has been shut down! Shuttered forever! In Christ, God has done what your hard work couldn't: made a sinner like you righteous. He has sown you on good, fertile soil and has sent his Spirit to dwell within you. He has finished the work and accomplished the goal of your salvation. "For those who live according to the flesh set their minds on the things of the flesh, but those who live according to the Spirit set their minds on the things of the Spirit. For to set the mind on the flesh is death, but to set the mind on the Spirit is life and peace." That is absolutely true. But take comfort. God has acted. In Christ, you are in the Spirit. In Christ, you have life and peace. What first seemed difficult (be careful what kind of seed you are) became impossible (the Sower is in charge of the seeds) and then, counterintuitively, the impossible became peaceful (you are sown on fertile soil). Going the other way and following our human instinct to reinterpret the impossible as merely difficult puts the responsibility right back on you, destroys your peace, and ruins everything.

LOST IN RE-TRANSLATION

In general, I'm a lover of social media. I enjoy being able to keep up with those people that I can't see in person, and I'm normally pretty immune to the negative effects of online connectivity. I do have a lot of Christian friends on social media, though—as you might imagine—and one of the things that does get under my skin is the rampant re-translation of the Bible that people engage in, I suppose in an effort to give "an encouraging word" to each other. You've seen the posts I mean—they're words posted over a seascape, or a sunset, or a mountain vista. They don't normally encourage me, though...in fact, I usually cringe. For instance, I saw a post recently that featured a beautifully cloudy evening sky with the words "When you've done everything you can do, that's when God will step in and do what you can't do." That seems like a relatively innocuous Footprints-in-the-Sand-style sentiment, right? Not quite Gospel truth (as we discussed in Chapter 3), but not the worst thing ever. But then I saw that it came with a Scripture reference: 2 Corinthians 12:10. I was confused. Wait, did the Bible actually say that? Would *the Apostle Paul* have penned such a thing? It sent me scrambling for my Bible. Here's what I found when I opened the ESV: "For the sake of Christ, then, I am content with weaknesses, insults, hardships, persecutions, and calamities. For when I am weak, then I am strong." Wow. Quite a bit different, wouldn't you say?

This verse comes immediately following Paul's discussion of the thorn that God has given him in the flesh, to "keep [him] from becoming conceited." Paul begs for this thorn to be taken away, but God tells him that it will stay, and God gives him an incredible dose of Gospel Good News to soothe his pain: "My grace is sufficient for you, for my power is made perfect in weakness" (2 Cor. 12:9a). What a different message this is than what I saw plastered over the evening sky on Instagram! Far from being a promise that God will pick up where you leave off, that he will be the second baton-carrier in the relay race of your life, this is a promise that God will use the difficulties of your life to show his strength. "Difficulties" is, in fact, not nearly a strong enough word. Look at the language Paul uses! Weaknesses, insults, hardships, persecutions, calamities. In another word: death. God is using the deaths of your daily existence to show that he is the only source of real life. He will be God when you are merely human. He will succeed where you fail. He brings possible out of impossible. In this re-translation, we have gone from life being impossible ("a thorn was given me in the flesh, a messenger of Satan to harass me") to life being difficult ("When you've done everything you can do, that's when God will step in and do what you can't do").

In the "new" version, impossible has been made difficult and, again, everything is ruined. God becomes a break-glass-in-case-of-emergency helper, not the very sustaining force of life.

JESUS WILL ONLY BE YOUR EVERYTHING

Imagine with me, for a moment, that you're at the beach. It's a nice, warm day, and the water is crystal clear. There are some pretty big waves, but they don't scare you…they're mostly just beautiful to look at. You're out swimming, just drifting around, playing with the undertow like it's not a big deal when, all of a sudden, you realize that you're out further than you thought you were, the waves are bigger than you're prepared for, your feet can't reach the bottom, and there's no one around. You're actually really far from the shore, you notice, and you feel really tired. All of a sudden, the surf becomes unmanageable. Wave after wave crashes down on you, pushing you under the surface and you realize that you're in some trouble. You try to keep your head above water, but it gets harder and harder to swim back up after you're pushed under. On a couple of occasions, you can't quite get back to the surface before you need to take a breath, and you get a mouthful of brackish water instead. It seems crazy to think that you might drown, because you can see the bright sun, and because just a few minutes ago everything seemed fine, but the pounding of the surf drowns out all other sound, and your body just can't seem to do what you want it to. More sea water forces its way into your mouth. That's when panic sets in. Drowning, something you'd literally never thought of before, now seems eerily inevitable.

But then, there's another sound competing with the crashing waves, a rhythmic thumping that's accompanied by a dark shadow and a great wind. And then, seemingly out of nowhere, a white life preserver ring plops into the water next to you. It's the most beautiful thing you've ever seen. You go, in that instant, from being sure you're going to drown to being assured of your salvation. Weakly, you reach out for the life ring and hold on for dear life as you're lifted out of the sea, up into the rescue helicopter, and back to the beach and to safety.

An hour or so later, you're being interviewed by the local news about the incident. "So you thought your life was over!" they say. "What happened? How were you saved?" And it's at this point, that, like any normal person, you take some of the credit for yourself.

"Well, a big thank-you goes, of course, to the lifeguards at the beach, the Coast Guard, and especially the EMTs who pumped all the water out of my lungs, but I have to say that the most critical moment of the whole incident was when the life ring landed in the water next to me and I had to decide whether to grab hold of it or not. I should get a little credit—don't you think?—for making such a good decision there."

Of course, that's ridiculous. No one would ever say such a thing. And yet, when we talk about our Christian salvation, almost every one of us wants to reserve a little credit for ourselves. "A little credit" is our addiction. We know not to take all of it... we know that Jesus is the savior, but didn't we do a little bit? Don't we talk about it as the best decision we ever made? Didn't we have to respond? Didn't we have to give our lives to Christ? Didn't we have to go one yard after Jesus went ninety-nine? Weren't we the ones who had to ask him into our hearts? Even Jesus says in Revelation that he's standing at the door knocking...don't we have to actually open the door? Didn't we have to reach out for the life preserver? Don't we get...a little credit?

There's a tiny little two-verse story in Luke 17 (vv. 5-6) that serves as Jesus' giant assault on the idea of "a little credit." The disciples come to Jesus and ask him to increase their faith. At first glance, this seems like—at worst—a benign request and at best a sort of laudable one. Isn't it a good thing to want more faith? Not, apparently, according to Jesus. He responds with a verbal smackdown: "If you had faith like a grain of mustard seed, you could say to this mulberry tree, 'Be uprooted and planted in the sea,' and it would obey you." In Matthew 17, he says that that same tiny faith—if it existed—could move mountains. Why does he react so harshly? He's not, as some people think, speaking encouragingly, as if to spur people on to have more faith and to move their life's metaphorical mountains. He is pointing out just how little faith they have! Remember our propensity to want a little credit? Jesus knows that propensity, and he won't stand for it. Jesus is the doctor giving us the diagnosis that we've been hiding from ourselves. He tells us the truth, no matter how painful it is. He will not be the person who gives you a little more of what you already have. He insists on being *all* you have. When you catch yourself in the disciples' shoes, thinking that you're doing well but could stand to do better, remember the Sermon on the Mount.

Remember that one? (For reference, the following excerpts are from Matthew 5.)

> "You have heard that it was said, 'An eye for an eye and a tooth for a tooth.' But I say to you, Do not resist the one who is evil. But if anyone slaps you on the right cheek, turn to him the other also... (vv. 38-39)

> "You have heard that it was said to those of old, 'You shall not murder; and whoever murders will be liable to judgment.' But I say to you that everyone who is angry with his brother will be liable to judgment; ... and whoever says, 'You fool!' will be liable to the hell of fire... (vv. 21-22)

> "You therefore must be perfect, as your heavenly Father is perfect." (v. 48)

Inherent in the request to have more faith is the idea that we already have some faith of our own. Jesus takes us back to square one: outside of him, we have no faith at all. Inherent in the idea that we could stand to get better is that we're already pretty good. Outside of him, *we aren't even alive.* In other words, our situation isn't difficult. It's not merely life-threatening. Our situation is impossible: we're dead.

See, my drowning swimmer story was a bit of a trick: we think we're a drowning swimmer; Jesus says we're dead. He refuses even to give us the chance to brag about grabbing the life preserver. He shows us that we need so much more than a rescue; we need a resurrection. The law is how he shows us that we're dead and the Sermon on the Mount is a perfect example. The difficult laws of "You have heard it said..." make us think we're drowning. The impossible laws of "But I say to you..." show us a harsher truth: that we're dead. "Therefore you must be perfect" is the final nail in the coffin.

In Ephesians 2:1-6, St. Paul says this, and couldn't be more blunt about it: "You were dead in trespasses and sins." Boom. Dead. As far as the ability to please God goes, you're flatlined. It's over. You're dead. But, praise God, he's not finished! "You were dead in trespasses and sins, but God, being rich in mercy, because of the great love with which he loved us, even when we were dead in our trespasses, made us alive together with Christ—by grace you have been saved—and raised us up with him and seated us with him in the heavenly places." Listen: the Christian story is not a story of a narrow escape from the jaws of death. Ours is a story of actual death and total resurrection!

Jesus refuses to be our helper. He refuses to be our coach. He refuses to be that final thing that pushes us over the top to greatness. He refuses to be the top-up on our tank of faith. He refuses to be the great marathon to which we must add only one step. He will not be the ninety-nine yards. In fact, he will not even wait for you answer the door. Listen to Romans 5: "For while we were still weak, at the right time Christ died for the ungodly…God shows his love for us in that while we were still sinners, Christ died for us" (vv. 6, 8). While we are desperately closing latches and throwing deadbolts and shouting, "No thanks! Come back another time! I'm not home!" through the door…this is when God sends his son to and for us. Yes, Jesus is standing there knocking, as the book of Revelation attests. But his knock is cracking the planks, busting the locks, and tearing off the hinges. Your door is coming down; his love for you cannot be contained. When Christ's knocking is over, and the door is lying in smithereens on the floor, all we can do is meekly say, "Come in, you're all I have." It is into that surrender that he says, "Yes, I am all you have. And I am all you need."

When the life preserver ring lands next to you in that turbulent ocean, there's no weighing of options. There's no thinking twice. It is the most beautiful thing you've ever seen. When Jesus' disciples come to him and ask him to increase their faith, Jesus needs to help them understand the true nature of their problem. It's not that they don't have enough faith. It's that they don't realize that they need saving. We often don't either. And so we come to Jesus, asking for more faith. Or asking him to be our helper. Or our coach. Our ninety-nine yards. And Jesus will not have it. He will only be your everything. If you had any faith at all, you could move mountains. Do you want to go outside and try it? Put the book down, I'll wait.

It's difficult for a drowning swimmer to reach out for the life preserver ring. But our problem is more profound: we're no longer drowning...we've drowned. In terms of faith, we are dead. But even our death is not the end of the story: "But God, being rich in mercy, because of the great love with which he loved us, even when we were dead in our trespasses, made us alive together with Christ—by grace you have been saved." Jesus is our everything.

FEAR THE REAPER

Jim Valvano was the coach of one of the most famous teams in the history of college basketball, the 1983 North Carolina State Wolfpack, a team that won the NCAA Championship that year in amazing fashion. He's probably more known, though, for his emotional speech at the first ESPY awards, shortly before his death from cancer. The odd thing about Jim Valvano's death, though, is that no one thought he was actually going to die. I recently rewatched the ESPN *30 for 30* documentary *Survive and Advance*, which chronicled that 1983 team's NCAA run. But more interesting to me than the basketball, though, was how the film treated Valvano's diagnosis, struggle, and eventual death.

Almost every person interviewed in the film, from Valvano's players to his wife and friends, said that when they first heard that Jim had been diagnosed with cancer, they just knew that he would beat it. He was a fighter, they all agreed, and he would win. This is the language we use with cancer: the language of victory. I saw a post on Facebook recently in which a young boy wanted 100,000 "likes" because he'd "beaten" cancer. The people in Valvano's life all spoke of their surprise as he became sicker, and then their shock at his death. They'd really and honestly, it turned out, despite all rationality, thought he would win. We use this victory language to try to convince ourselves that a win over death is like a win for the '83 Wolfpack: facing long odds, but not impossible.

Even Jim Valvano died. The winner of all those NCAA tournament games didn't win. He couldn't win the ultimate one. The Facebook boy might have beaten cancer, but he hasn't beaten death. No mere human has, or ever will.

As humans, we want to win everything, but the victory we most want to garner is the one with the biggest stakes: we want to defeat our own deaths. The incredible and profound thing about Jesus' cross is that it doesn't shrink back from death. It doesn't avoid it. Christ's cross looks death in the face and boldly confronts it. The cross is the end of the human contest. Everyone loses. As the Doors said, "No one here gets out alive."

Bill Simmons, a former ESPN personality (and, perhaps tellingly, one of the creators and executive producers of the *30 for 30* series), gave voice to this tension in an episode of his "The Bill Simmons Podcast" on December 16, 2016, discussing the then-recent death of TNT basketball sideline reporter Craig Sager. Here's what he said: "I was surprised by just how shocked I was that somebody who had been battling cancer for three years couldn't beat it. And I think that's part of the legacy of Sager, which is that the dude was such a fighter. I was surprised that cancer beat him. Cancer beats everybody…I just kept assuming he was going to keep fighting and fighting…I can't remember a public figure fighting harder than that guy did to live."

He says it so clearly: cancer beats everybody, and yet he—for some reason—assumed that Craig Sager would be the exception. Simmons had unknowingly made the impossible—the defeat of death—possible in his mind. But that's the thing about human life: the diagnosis is terminal for all of us. Fight or no fight, we all die.

Only God, in Christ, brings victory out of defeat. God, in Christ, brings life out of death. We all die. Yes, it's true, and unavoidable. In Christ, though, we do not die without hope. In fact, we have something even better than hope; we have a promise: new and eternal life.

FROM DOCTRINES TO PRECEPTS

Jesus was well aware of our propensity to make the move from impossible to difficult. He simply won't let us do it. When he sits down for a meal with the Pharisees, he gets a perfect opportunity to make sure. During the meal, the Pharisees notice something interesting, something that they find disgusting: Jesus isn't making his disciples wash their hands! So, they ask Jesus why his disciples are not following the traditions of the elders, which involved significant, serious ceremonial hand-washing, and the extra cleaning of all the stuff with which they cooked and ate. In response, Jesus quotes Isaiah to them: "'This people honors me with their lips, but their heart is far from me; in vain do they worship me, teaching as doctrines the commandments of men.' You abandon the commandment of God and hold to human tradition" (Matthew 15:8-9 from Isaiah 29:13).

This is meaty stuff, but valuable. In fact, it's one of Jesus' favorite topics: the inside vs. the outside, and which is more important. He talks about it all the time. Jesus accuses the Pharisees of "honoring [him] with their lips" but being far from him in their hearts. Lips: outside. Hearts: inside. The outside gives off an appearance that is not borne out by the inside. Jesus is clearly claiming that the lip-service (and this is exactly the sort of situation from which that phrase came) given to him by the Pharisees is worthless. What he wants is their hearts, and that's what he's not getting.

He goes on: "In vain do they worship me, teaching as doctrines the commandments of men." This is an interesting one. What does it mean to say that they are teaching human precepts, human rules, as doctrines? Well, let's take the hand-washing example. God's law is "be clean." The Pharisees turn that into "wash your hands for half an hour before every meal." They turn the impossible into the difficult. And then, they forget about the original doctrine, true cleanliness, and only focus on the hand-washing thing. Let's use an example that makes a little more sense to us. God's command is "don't lust after someone who isn't your wife." Over the years, religious groups have turned this into precepts like, "Women can't wear dresses that show more than their ankles" or "Women must keep their heads covered at all times" or "Men and women cannot sit together at meals."

This is the *Footloose* syndrome: we turn God's law into a set of human rules, and then teach the human rules as if they were God's law. *Honor your father and mother* is hard…how about "call your parents once a week, and don't put them in a home until they're seventy?" *Thou shalt not steal* is hard…how about "don't cheat on your taxes enough to get audited." *Love thy neighbor* is hard…how about "unless they play Whitesnake songs at three in the morning." There's a great Derek Webb song called "A New Law" which includes the line, "What's the use in trading a law you can never keep for one you can that cannot get you anything?" This is exactly what the Pharisees were doing, and it is exactly what we do every day. We can't take the full weight of the actual law ("Be perfect" or "Love the Lord your God with all your heart, soul, mind, and strength, and love your neighbor as yourself"), so we translate it to something we can take: Call your mother every week, don't cheat too much on your taxes, and be nice to your neighbors. When I was in college, our new law was to have a quiet time every day and to avoid looking at pornography on the Internet. If you could do that, then you were doing well. We turned the whole of God's law into just that! The sad thing, of course, was that we couldn't even do that, much less love God and love our neighbor as ourselves.

After admonishing the Pharisees about treating human rules as though they were the law of God, Jesus turns to the actual law of God. The Pharisees are complaining that because of dirt on their hands, Jesus' disciples aren't clean. They're not being faithful to God. Jesus turns around and says, "You want to talk about unfaithful? You want to talk about unclean? Let's talk about unclean!" And then he says this:

> "Hear me, all of you, and understand: There is nothing outside a person that by going into him can defile him, but the things that come out of a person are what defile him. … For from within, out of the heart of man, come evil thoughts, sexual immorality, theft, murder, adultery, coveting, wickedness, deceit, sensuality, envy, slander, pride, foolishness. All these evil things come from within, and they defile a person." (Mark 7:14-15, 21-23)

Now, at first, it doesn't seem that this can possibly be right! I mean, remember Ephesians 6:12-17! "For we do not wrestle against flesh and blood, but against the rulers, against the authorities, against the cosmic powers over this present darkness, against the spiritual forces of evil in the heavenly places. Therefore take up the whole armor of God." You know the list: belt of truth, breastplate of righteousness, shield of faith, helmet of salvation. This is what we like. We're okay, and we put on the armor of God to protect us from the evil that is *out there!*

So what is Jesus talking about? We feel like he ought to be saying, "The world is an evil place. If you let it get into you it will defile you, so put on the whole armor of God. Protect yourself!" But that's not at all what he says, of course. Instead, he says, "The things that go into you" (the things that you experience or participate in) cannot make you unclean. This news is both good and bad. The good part is that you can do whatever you want. But the bad part is that you can't do whatever you want and stay clean. "Clean" is a lost cause for you. Jesus says the uncleanliness comes from inside you: it's your intentions. He says that "it is from within, from the human heart, that evil intentions come." Gulp. This is the law we'd like to trade in. We don't want the law to be about our hearts. We want to be able to say, "Well, I didn't actually *do* anything!" I just imagined throwing her under a bus. I just fantasized about slapping him across the face. I didn't actually act on it! Shouldn't that count for something? And, of course, it does. I'm sure your family members are all glad that you've been able to resist slapping them all the times you've wanted to. But as far as being clean goes? As far as your cleanliness before a holy God goes? Being righteous? We get no points for keeping our wicked thoughts to ourselves. We get no points for pretending that the impossible is merely difficult.

But! But there is the armor of God. And in redefining where sin and uncleanliness come from (from the heart; from inside you), Jesus redefines the armor of God. Rather than protecting you from threats without, it covers you against the disease within. We have the belt of truth around our waists, and are wearing the breastplate of righteousness. As shoes for our feet we proclaim the gospel of peace. We're holding the shield of faith, and have on our heads the helmet of salvation, and are holding onto the sword of the Spirit with every ounce of strength we've got. This is what God sees when he looks at us now. Where once there was sexual immorality, theft, murder, adultery, coveting, wickedness, deceit, sensuality, envy, slander, pride, foolishness, there is now truth, righteousness, peace, faith, and salvation. The whole armor of God is Jesus himself. When wearing him, we can do, eat, say, and think whatever we want and know that, though we are desperately unclean, we are wearing truth, righteousness, peace, faith, and best of all, salvation.

YOU'RE THE BIOLOGY FROG

We make this unwarranted transition—from impossible to difficult—because we are convinced that we are the leading men and women in the dramas of our lives. We are the actors responsible for the action...and therefore, that action had better be possible! But this isn't how the Bible thinks of us at all.

In the book of Hebrews we find a sentence that seems like it might fit pretty well into a high school biology textbook: "For the word of God is living and active, sharper than any two-edged sword, piercing to the division of soul and of spirit, of joints and of marrow, and discerning the thoughts and intentions of the heart" (4:12). Do you remember doing dissection in class? The frog (or fetal pig, or whatever) was laid out before you, and you had a scalpel in your hand. You were in charge, and you were going to find out what was going on inside that frog. Often, we approach the Bible in the same way. We think of the Bible as basically dead, lying there before us. It's up to us to figure out what's going on in there. But Hebrews (i.e. the

Bible itself) has a different message: the word of God is living and active. When we read the Bible, it's God's word that is in charge and that is holding the scalpel, not us. We're not the interpreter; the Word is. The Bible is not the dissection frog in high school biology, lying dead on the table. It's alive. In fact, *it's dissecting us*. We are the frog getting dissected.

We are the *object* of the cosmic drama of life, not the subject. We are the acted-upon, not the actor. If we are the actor, the urge to make things difficult—instead of impossible—makes sense. After all, if it was actually *Mission: Impossible*, the sequels would get boring pretty fast: another failed mission. But if we're not the star—and the true star delights in accomplishing the impossible—then there's no reason to lower the bar. Most of us, though, want that bar lowered, for a simple reason: it allows us to think that we might be capable of saving ourselves.

CHAPTER 8

YOUR DIFFICULT SAVIOR IS YOU

Remember my story about that awful high school high jump experience? When you think that a thing (a certain height in the high jump is just a convenient stand-in for any of the "hurdles" or "challenges to overcome" you have in your own life) is difficult but not impossible, you don't rely on anyone but yourself. Remember Chapter 1...we always do the hard thing. We love it. We want it. We think succeeding, on our own, at something difficult will make us look good. Unfortunately, though, difficult is rare and impossible is everywhere. This leads inevitably to failure. Self-salvation, in any lasting sense, never works. Only calling out for a savior *who is not you* results in actual salvation.

THE KEYS TO YOUR REDEMPTION

I'm sure you remember the rise and fall of Lance Armstrong. A gifted athlete and perhaps the greatest cyclist of all time, Armstrong became even more beloved for his defeat of cancer and his "Livestrong" foundation that raises money to combat that awful disease. His fall, of course, was due to his use of performance-enhancing steroids throughout his cycling career, a practice he vigorously denied for years. Finally, he admitted using the drugs on an episode of *Oprah* and began trying to rehabilitate his public image. Shortly after Armstrong spoke to Oprah, *The Wall Street Journal* ran a piece (by Reed Albergotti and Vanessa O'Connell) called "Behind Lance Armstong's Decison to Talk" which described a conversation that Armstrong had with the then-head of USADA (the United States Anti-Doping Agency), Travis Tygart. It is an incredible example of a man engaged in self-salvation:

> "You don't hold the keys to my redemption," [Armstrong] said, according to the person familiar with the meeting. "There's one person who holds the keys to my redemption," he went on, pointing at himself, "and that's me."

Tygart is said to have responded with just two words: "That's [expletive]." We should all agree. Armstrong thought his situation was difficult, and therefore assumed he could hold the keys to his own redemption. But that's [expletive], to borrow Tygart's language. Our situations are impossible, and we need a savior who is not us.

SELF-SALVATION AT THE END

As part of my ordination process, I was required to complete a section of Clinical Pastoral Education (CPE). This normally involves a certain number of hours spent in a clinical setting as a kind of volunteer chaplain trainee. I did my CPE at the VA hospital in Pittsburgh. Boiled down to its basic components, the program asks not-yet-ordained students to act as chaplains to the sick, the very sick, and the dying, and to process in group discussion sections the feelings that are brought up by the experience. It's very much being thrown into the deep end of the pastoral pool and finding out if you can swim.

One conversation—and subsequent debriefing session—that I had that summer has stuck with me in a very powerful way ever since. It wouldn't be an exaggeration to say that this one conversation has informed my entire pastoral approach.

This was a day like any other. I was tasked, walking around in the clerical collar that I hadn't yet earned, with going into hospital rooms and relating to the people whom I found there. Comforting them, praying with them, giving them whatever pastoral care they needed. This particular room was a normal room on a normal hallway, and the interaction started normally enough. I walked in, and a man was sitting up in the bed. Just like usual. So I said, brightly, "How are you today?"

"Well, son," the man said, not interested in beating around the bush, "not too well. I'm dying."

I froze. I couldn't believe it. It was so stark, like a slap in the face. I was completely unprepared and I didn't have any idea what to say. It's funny: though it's quite true that I remember almost every aspect of this interaction down to the finest detail, and I've thought about it hundreds of times since, I cannot remember the next words out of my mouth. I must have said something, though, even if it was just a confused gurgle. Perhaps I was able to choke out something like, "How do you feel about that?" because the man responded, and his next words will remain seared into my brain for the rest of my life: "I think I've lived a good life. I'm just not sure it was good enough." His words were a perfect echo of James Ryan's words at the end of *Saving Private Ryan*: "Tell me I've been a good man."

Can you imagine the suffering? The fear? This worry is burden enough for those of us somewhere near the middle of our lives, but to come to the end and to not know if the life you've lived has been "good enough" is enough to make me want to cry, fifteen years later.

Then, a miracle happened. I found myself able to speak, and

inexplicably given things to say. I told the man that his situation was exactly why Jesus had come. Our savior came for those of us whose lives weren't "good enough." We talked for a few minutes about sin, forgiveness, and redemption in Christ Jesus, and then I left the room, elated and thankful to God that I'd been given an opportunity to proclaim the Good News about Jesus to a dying man who needed to hear it.

My elation wasn't to last long. That afternoon, in our group discussion, I presented this interaction, and the group—along with the full-time, already-ordained chaplains at the hospital—gave me feedback. Everyone felt I'd handled the situation incorrectly. Instead, the group thought, I should have reassured the man that his life *had* been good enough. In their opinion, the best way to care for this man would have been to try to convince him that his fears were unfounded. There's a significant problem with this strategy, though: there's no way he would have believed me if I had told him that. When someone tells you that thing that you know they think you want to hear, you smile ruefully, nod, and go on believing exactly what you believed before. When the girl dumping you says, "It's not you, it's me," you don't believe her. It might be nice to hear in the very short term, but it's not going to console you during those long, lonely nights.

The man in that hospital bed thought that he had to be his own savior. He thought he had to be "good enough" to earn his eternal reward. This is not the Christian story. Our God doesn't lie to us. He doesn't say, "It's not you, it's me." He doesn't say, "No, no, your life has been just fine!" or its analog, "I love you just the way you are." God knows that we are great sinners; he had to send his only son to die for us! We're not fine just the way we are, and that man at the VA Hospital had most assuredly not lived a life that was good enough to earn him a trip through the pearly gates. His fear was based on the fact that—though he probably wouldn't have said it so bluntly—he was his own (failed) savior. The Christian Gospel is thankfully much better news than "save yourself." Our Good News is of a perfect savior who comes to save the imperfect and needy people who need him most.

PATHETIC AND POWERFUL

One of the greatest documentaries I've ever seen is *Murderball*, the story of the United States Quad-Rugby team, a Paralympic team of quadriplegics. "Quads," as they call themselves, refers to the fact that they have lost some use of all four limbs. Almost none of the rugby players have any use of their legs, but many have relatively little impairment in their arms. The level of impairment depends on where the neck or back was broken. "Murderball" is the nickname for wheelchair rugby, which teams play in modified chairs that look like something out of *Mad Max*.

One of the more interesting things about the film is the interplay between physical disability and mental attitude. As you might imagine, the quadriplegics who play murderball are some of the most competitive, independent, and feisty spirits in the world. They would kill themselves before letting anyone take pity on them. One of the players, Mark Zupan, says, "I'll go up to people and start talking (expletive). And they'll look at me like they don't know what to do. And I'll say, 'What, you don't want to hit a kid in a chair?' (Expletive) hit me! I'll hit you back!" Zupan is clearly starting these altercations to prove his self-sufficiency and strength because he is afraid of being seen as weak and needy.

Of course, no one can be more quickly forgiven for this sort of overcompensation than these guys. I can't imagine the struggles that they have gone and continue to go through. The film, though, makes the juxtaposition impossible to ignore: feelings of weakness (the film begins with a painfully long scene of Zupan simply getting dressed) lead to professions of strength. These professions, though, are offset starkly by another moment in the film. Scott Hogsett, one of Zupan's teammates, is talking about picking up girls: "The more pitiful I am, the more the women like me!" Beyond the obvious disingenuity of Hogsett's strategy, it's interesting to note that he is claiming, in effect, to be pretending to be pathetic. Even though he calls himself "pitiful"—something Zupan would never do—he's in fact making the opposite claim: he's not pitiful, he's just pretending in order to get the girl.

How do you handle your deep-seated sufferings? Do we, knowing that Christ came to and for sufferers, wear the thorns in our flesh as badges of honor? Or are we keeping our needs deep beneath our surface, in the subconscious hope that when Jesus comes, we'll be able to say, "I'm doing just fine on my own, thanks"? If it's true that sufferers will, in Christ, lack nothing (James 1), why do we work so hard to seem just fine?

In a profound sense, I understand Mark Zupan and Scott Hogsett. I'm ready for a fight. Aren't you? We want to be able to stand before Jesus and say, "Lord, you know I'm not perfect! Look, I've suffered. My family is broken; my self-esteem is low. I'm not confined to a wheelchair…but I am weak. It was a long, tough road, and I'm a little woozy." We might even quote "Footprints in the Sand": "You even had to carry me sometimes. But the important thing is, I made it! Here I am."

The thing that Jesus needs us to give up is the thing we hold onto most tightly: our hearts, our very lives. Jesus said, "If anyone would come after me, let him deny himself and take up his cross and follow me. For whoever would save his life will lose it, but whoever loses his life for my sake and the gospel's will save it." (Mark 8:34-35).

We're willing to let Jesus carry us part of the way. We're willing to be helped, but we want to be our own savior. We will accept a helping hand, but not a savior from outside of ourselves. What we can't abide is dying...which is exactly what relying on a savior who is not you entails! For us, dying means failure. It means the end. We're used to hearing that someone "lost the fight" against cancer. We think of dying as losing! This is why we pick fights from our wheelchairs. But Jesus says, "You need to give up on that old heart, that fighting spirit! It's the source of sin! It's the very thing that's holding you back!" But there is good news. Paul writes in 2 Corinthians that "if anyone is in Christ, he is a new creation. The old has passed away; behold, the new has come." The old heart has been removed. Not rehabilitated; removed and replaced. Death, for us, is not the end, but the beginning, of life. And so we might sing the great chorus of the Third Day song "Take My Life":

> Please take from me my life
> When I don't have the strength
> To give it away to you, Jesus

We don't have the strength, but we're full of fight. It's this fight—this desire to save ourselves—that Jesus ultimately has to kill. He must be our savior. Jesus takes the hearts we refuse to give him, and behold, all things have become new.

SELF-SALVATION KILLS COMPASSION

When you see people as basically able to save themselves—or to improve their situations—it makes compassion impossible. I learned this permanently when I was in college, though not in the classroom. A classmate of mine was having sex with her boyfriend and wanted to stop, in an effort to return to sexual purity. She would come to me each time they succumbed to their sexual impulses, hoping that by confessing—and having me "hold her accountable"—she would be inspired to stop doing the thing that she so desperately wanted to stop doing. I'll never forget what happened. At first, I was able to be the compassionate shoulder-to-cry-on that she needed. I prayed for her, hoped for her, and tried to help her through her struggle. But as the confessions became *more* frequent instead of less, my compassion began to dry up. I began to resent her. Why couldn't she just stop? Why couldn't she and her boyfriend just keep their clothes on? I mean, seriously. If you don't want to have sex with someone, just don't. It didn't seem that hard to me. (I was comically blind to my own nature…as, of course, I remain to this day.) I couldn't understand how someone could continually do something that she didn't want to do (Romans 7:14-20). It is a miracle, in retrospect, that I didn't completely ruin my relationship with that friend. It wasn't until years later, when I learned that life was impossible, rather than just difficult, that I understood the pain, fear, and guilt that she had been living through.

Here's a sadder, but no less relevant story: that of Junior Seau. I remember being at an open gym several years ago, shooting baskets with a bunch of guys, talking about the news of the day: the apparent (at the time) suicide of former NFL great and presumptive Hall of Famer Seau. Many of the guys couldn't believe that a man who was so famous, so rich, and who had so much could be depressed. What could possibly be so bad about his life that it wasn't worth living? The tone of the conversation quickly became derisive. Seau must have been weak. Fragile. Pathetic. Then, almost hesitantly, someone suggested that his brain may have been irreparably damaged by the numerous minor head traumas he suffered over the course of his playing career.

It was like a switch was thrown. All of a sudden, no one

had a cutting remark. No one was talking about how satisfied they were with so much less than Seau had. We recalled the story of Dave Duerson, another former NFL player who committed suicide, who had shot himself in the chest expressly so that his brain could be studied; he had known his depression was physically sourced (subsequent medical examination of his brain proved him right). The mood in the gym became somber, and the tone, compassionate.

I couldn't believe how quickly derision had become compassion. Then I realized what had really happened: the group had collectively transitioned from seeing Seau as basically "able," that is, in control of and responsible for his actions and mental state, to basically "disabled," that is, the victim of forces beyond his control. It is only natural to feel derision for people who are able to control themselves and do not, and just as natural to feel compassion for people who are unable to control themselves.

Here's the thing: Christians are disabled. Not especially disabled, just *as* disabled as non-Christians. My college friend was disabled. I am disabled. All people are, in this way, disabled. It is easy for us to think of Christians as "able" in a way that they (and we) are not. And the result of this mistaken thinking? Derision. If we see people as fundamentally able to make good choices, possessing the ability to improve, and able to control their minds, our ability to be compassionate toward them will wither and die. This will damage—and threaten to kill—any relationship.

As a pastor, I have come to know not only that Paul's words in Romans 7 ("I do not do what I want, but I do the very thing I hate") are true, but that seeing them as part of a universal human condition is fundamental to pastoral care for people. We could call this condition something like "Impossible Life Syndrome." We're all sufferers. Compassion cannot exist where we see people as "able," because people are inveterate failures. Pastors will either come to hate their people (because they're not following your good advice) or themselves (because you're not communicating the advice well enough). In either case, hatred is the end result. And, of course, the situation is as precarious for friends as it is for pastors.

If we are to avoid hating those closest to us (including ourselves!), and are to avoid heaping scorn on those further away, we must begin to see people as the "disabled" creatures that they are. Like Paul, my college friend, Junior Seau, and me, they often do the very thing they hate. We can only be there, compassionately, when they cry out for a savior, with the Good News that there is now no condemnation for those in Christ Jesus (Romans 8:1).

We assume that other people are "able" because we are desperate to claim that we ourselves are able. It is only when we can admit that we are disabled—and that everyone else is just like us—that compassion can begin to bloom. After all, we say, "I'm only human" to excuse our mistakes, don't we? Let's begin believing it, and the disability that it entails.

There is no peace to be gained by lowering the high jump bar. When impossible is watered down to difficult, we smirkingly and confidently pass on all the lower heights, only to find ourselves crashing and burning. Our planned hymn, "I Made It! Here I Am!" is tragically modulated into "I'm Just Not Sure It Was Good Enough." We can never be sure. Better, then, to admit the truth: our lives our impossible.

CHAPTER 9

FROM DIFFICULT TO IMPOSSIBLE

Unfortunately for the believer in human ability, it turns out—as we've seen—that impossible is everywhere. Why is that? Here's a simple way to think about it: the law of God is a picture of God. God is love, so he commands us to love. God is faithful, so he expects fidelity from his people. God is good, righteous, and just, so his creation ought to conform to that mold.

There's a reason that the sneaking suspicion that we're not good enough is common to all people, of any race, religion, or nation. The reason isn't complex: there is a perfect creator God of the universe, whether a certain person knows of him, believes in him, swears allegiance to him, or not. If he exists, his existence is not dependent on the opinion of his creation. He is perfect, and so the itch of perfection irritates each one of us in the deep recesses of our brains. We know that perfection is out there, and we can tell—again, whether we admit it or not—that we're not perfect. Most of us, in fact, *do* admit it, even if it's in the context of comparing ourselves favorably to someone else: "I'm not perfect," we'll acknowledge, "but at least I'm better than *him*."

If we're willing to admit that we're not perfect and we can see—to our great chagrin—that God's requirement is that we must be (Matthew 5:48 again), we ought not to fall prey to the temptation to lower the bar. As we saw in the last chapter, there is no peace there. We think that if we just make things a little bit easier—turn the impossible into the difficult—we'll be able to rest. But it turns out that it's not true. In fact, the opposite is true. When things are difficult, we are always striving, and there is no rest. Let us, then, not lower the bar. Let us raise it! The law, as we've said, exists to show us our need for a savior. Let us let the law do its job, and illuminate the one who kept it for us.

HOW MANY COATS?

John the Baptist, preparing the way for the arrival of Jesus, in Luke 3, said, "Even now the axe is laid to the root of the trees. Every tree therefore that does not bear good fruit is cut down and thrown into the fire." Now that's some old-school preaching! John the Baptist came preaching hellfire and brimstone. He said that the time was coming! And the crowds (probably trembling) asked him, "What then shall we do?" The tax collectors (trembling) asked him, "What then shall we do?" The soldiers (yep, them too) asked him, "What then shall we do?" And John gives them the law, the rules, the requirements. He has new rules for life for every group: He tells the crowds that "whoever has two coats must share with anyone who has none; and whoever has food must do likewise" (NRSV). The tax collectors were supposed to "collect no more than the amount prescribed." And the soldiers: "Do not extort money from anyone by threats or false accusation, and be satisfied with your wages."

In their question, "What then shall we do?" you can feel the underlying fear. "Just tell me what I need to know to avoid this axe that is lying at the root of the trees! How can I avoid getting thrown into the fire?" And John gives them the law: share your coats and food and do your work honestly. Obey the law, and you'll be fine. Disobey? Not so much.

In my tradition (Anglicanism) and in many mainline traditions, this piece of Scripture is read right before Christmas. As a church, we're preparing for Jesus' incarnation—his coming to earth—so we read this passage about John announcing his coming into his earthly ministry. The association of this imagery—and this fire and brimstone sermon—with Christmas reminds me a lot of the first line of that one John Lennon song "Happy Christmas." Do you know it? Here's the line: "So this is Christmas...and what have you done?"

Isn't it a little jarring to begin a Christmas song with that line? A little intense, right? But John Lennon is right in line with John the Baptist, isn't he? And listen, under the law, it's entirely appropriate for John to tell the people, "The Son of God is coming! Get yourselves in order!" In other words, "So this is Christmas...and what have you done?" But I do think that there's something incomplete about the message that John (the Baptist, not Lennon) is preaching, and I think that John himself gives us a clue. After he tells the different groups of people what to do, he says, "I baptize you with water, but he who is mightier than I is coming, the strap of whose sandals I am not worthy to untie. He will baptize you with the Holy Spirit and fire" (v. 16). John is making it clear that he is not the one for whom they have been waiting. He's not the Messiah. Jesus is coming, and he is greater than John. He's different than John. It might be our default setting to assume that while John is here preaching the law, Jesus will come preaching the Gospel. However, I want to suggest to you that while John is preaching the law, he's not actually preaching the law as profoundly as Jesus will. In other words, his bad news isn't bad enough, and so he doesn't quite understand how good the good news is going to be.

Let's look for a moment at one of the laws that John preaches. John says, "Whoever has two coats must share with anyone who has none; and whoever has food must do likewise." Simple enough, right? But now look at how Jesus talks about coats. Jesus says, in Matthew 5, "If someone takes your cloak, do not stop him from taking your tunic. Give to everyone who asks you, and if anyone takes what belongs to you, do not demand it back." And there you have it: on the one hand we have John's law; a difficult law, but a law we can keep. You have an extra coat? Give it away. On the other we have Jesus' law; a law we can't keep. Someone steals your coat? Give them more. John thinks he's being so hardcore, right? "You brood of vipers! Who warned you to flee from the wrath to come?" And then with all that "axe lying at the root of the trees" stuff. But in the end, his law doesn't have nearly the teeth that Jesus' law does. So which one are you going for? Well, if you're anything like me, I'm going with John! Give me a difficult law any day. A law I can keep.

We like that new law (remember Derek Webb's distinction between two kinds of law in Chapter 7?) because the old law—Jesus' law—is about perfection. Perfection is totally that old law, that Old Testament law, "You shall love the LORD your God with *all* your heart and with *all* your soul and with *all* your might," and it's that Jesus law, too: "if anyone would sue you and take your coat, let him have your cloak as well.... You therefore," he says, "*must be perfect*, as your heavenly Father is perfect." John's not talking about perfection; he's talking about "pretty good." And "pretty good" we can get on board with! I'm fine with the idea of giving away my coat. Actually I like it...if I have two. It lets me feel good about myself, and lets me stay warm at the same time! I like feeling good about myself. Jesus, though, doesn't seem to want me to feel good about myself. He keeps saying things like, "Love your enemies, do good to those who hate you, bless those who curse you, pray for those who mistreat you. If someone strikes you on one cheek, turn to him the other also." Can't you just hear John's "new law" version of this? "Be polite to your enemies, stay away from those who curse you, and pray for those who mistreat you...as long as they don't keep doing it. If someone strikes you on the cheek, don't hit them back." Yes! That is a law I can keep! But it's not the law that Jesus is talking about.

And you can see, also, that John expected Jesus to preach the same kind of message he was preaching! Look at how he introduces him: "He who is mightier than I is coming, the strap of whose sandals I am not worthy to untie. He will baptize you with the Holy Spirit and fire. His winnowing fork is in his hand, to clear his threshing floor and to gather the wheat into his barn, but the chaff he will burn with unquenchable fire." John thinks Jesus is gonna be kickin' butt and takin' names! Unquenchable fire! But what John doesn't know is that Jesus is going to preach that old law, and what John doesn't seem to totally understand is that it's that old law that leads to the Gospel.

John is the last preacher who didn't have access to the Gospel. He pointed the way to Jesus—he knew to do that much, but he didn't quite understand what Jesus was going to do. John is the last preacher—at least in the Bible—who preached the law and then stopped. He's the guy who tried to save people by giving them something to do. But a few years later, while Jesus was around preaching, John sent a messenger to him: "Are you the one we've been waiting for? The Messiah? Or should we wait for another?" (Matthew 11:3). He's saying, "You're not doing it the way I thought you were going to be doing it!"

And Jesus *isn't* doing it the way John did. John makes the age-old mistake of turning the law into something we can keep. The tragedy is, John's law can't get us anything! Only perfection can save us. If we water down the law into something we can keep, we won't know we need the Gospel. We'll forget that only perfection will do. If we don't recognize that we're not perfect, we won't call out for the one who is.

Jesus, the "friend of sinners," the friend of the imperfect, takes the first step, and makes the law worse. He shows us our need. He shows us what "love your neighbor" really means. It means so much more than, "Eh, if you've got an extra coat, give it away to someone." "Love your neighbor" means nothing less than the profound words that make up the command. Actually love your neighbor as much as you love yourself. Who can stand in the face of such a demand?

See, we're afraid of a law we can't keep. And we should be. It makes our salvation dependent on someone else. That's scary. Except when that someone is Jesus. John announced the coming of someone more powerful than him. Thank goodness! John pointed the way to one, Jesus Christ, who would first preach an old law, but ultimately, not only preach the Gospel, but be the Gospel himself. The law shows us our need. It brings us into contact with our failings. It allows us to know the desperation for salvation. Turn the other cheek. Love your neighbor. Call out for a savior. The Good News is that Jesus Christ came to earth, to live and die as one of us, not to give us a new set of rules by which to save ourselves, but to be our salvation. That's why we don't ever have to be afraid. John thought that Jesus would come in judgment—"His winnowing fork is in his hand, to clear his threshing floor and to gather the wheat into his barn, but the chaff he will burn with unquenchable fire." He envisioned a totally different kind of Christmas…where the bad kids (that's you and me, lest we forget) get a much worse punishment than coal in our stockings; we'd get that unquenchable fire.

Want to know what Jesus actually said when he actually came? He said, "The Spirit of the Lord is upon me, because he has anointed me to proclaim good news to the poor. He has sent me to proclaim liberty to the captives and recovering of sight to the blind, to set at liberty those who are oppressed, to proclaim the year of the Lord's favor" (Luke 4:18-19).

John Lennon sang, "So this is Christmas...and what have you done?" The Gospel gives us a new song: "So this is Christmas, let us celebrate what Christ has done for us."

THE MAN I ALMOST AM

Most great films have a memorable line, something that you walk out of the theater saying to yourself and to your friends, and that you find popping up in the popular lexicon. Maybe if a movie truly captures the imagination of the public, it'll have two lines like that. I re-watched *Jerry Maguire* the other day and realized that that movie has three such lines in it, lines—and this is a movie that was made 20 years ago—that many people still use and quote today. The three lines are, of course, "You complete me," "You had me at hello," and "Show me the money." Incredible. Cameron Crowe deserves a lifetime achievement Oscar for those three sentences alone. But it's a fourth line from that movie that stood out to me on this viewing, and I bet it's one that's a little under your radar.

After Renée Zellweger's Dorothy Boyd has her first real date with Tom Cruise's Jerry Maguire, she's telling her sister about it the next morning...and really, she's telling her that she loves him. And she says this incredible thing: "I love him. I love him for the man he's trying to be. And I love him for the man he almost is."

Notice: she doesn't love him for who he is. She loves him for who he's trying to be. Doesn't this sound exactly like someone considering their New Year's resolutions?

How do you think of a new year dawning? If you're like

most people, you're thinking things like, This is the year that we can finally succeed. This is the year when we'll accomplish the things that we've so often failed to achieve in the past. So let's get to it! Each year, we make commitments to ourselves (and to others, and even, perhaps, to God) to be better than we were last year. Perhaps we want to finally lose that pesky fifteen pounds. Or fifty. Or we want to be more faithful in our Bible-reading and in our prayer lives. We want to finally put aside that besetting sin that's been plaguing us. A new year does seem like a good time for a fresh start.

But resolutions can be a tricky thing. In fact, hasn't joking about how quickly you're going to end up breaking your resolutions become more of a habit than the resolution-making itself? I envision St. Paul waking up on January 1, noticing all his Facebook friends' resolutions, and posting something along the lines of Galatians 3:

> O foolish Galatians! Who has bewitched you? It was before your eyes that Jesus Christ was publicly portrayed as crucified. Let me ask you only this: Did you receive the Spirit by works of the law or by hearing with faith? Are you so foolish? Having begun by the Spirit, are you now being perfected by the flesh? Did you suffer so many things in vain—if indeed it was in vain? Does he who supplies the Spirit to you and works miracles among you do so by works of the law, or by hearing with faith…? (v. 1-5)

See, New Year's resolutions are ways by which we try to cross the gulf between the us that we are today, and the us that we wish we were. When Dorothy Boyd says that she loves Jerry "for the man he's trying to become and for the man he almost is," that's all of us. We think that people—and God—won't really be able to love us until we're the us we're trying to become. So we resolve to get it done. But we Christians have already been given an eternal answer for the gulf that exists between the us that we are and the us that we ought to be! We read about it Philippians 2:6-8:

> ...though [Jesus] was in the form of God, [he] did
> not count equality with God a thing to be grasped,
> but emptied himself, by taking the form of a servant,
> being born in the likeness of men. And being found
> in human form, he humbled himself by becoming
> obedient to the point of death, even death on a cross.

Do you hear that? Jesus crossed the gulf between the us that we want to be and the us that we are, from that side to this side! Though he was God, he humbled himself, coming to us, and then humbled himself again, dying a criminal's death for the sins of the world. Paul sums it up even more clearly in Romans 3, when he says that "all have sinned...and are justified by his grace as a gift, through the redemption that is in Christ Jesus" (v. 23-24).

Doesn't the way we talk about resolutions often sound like an attempt to, as Paul put it in Galatians 3, be "perfected by the flesh?" "The righteousness of God has been manifested apart from the law," says Romans 3:21, and yet we take the turning of one year to another as our chance to give ourselves a new law: the law of the resolution.

So my answer used to be: Don't make resolutions. You'd be foolish to live under a law, knowing how the law works, and knowing that it necessarily results in failure and ultimately death. Now, though, I've got a new idea: make your resolutions harder.

The problem with your resolutions isn't that they're too hard for you to keep (though they usually are). The problem is that *you think you've got a chance.* The problem is that you've turned what ought to be impossible into merely difficult. So you rely on yourself, work up your will, exert all your effort, and give it your best shot. We think, perhaps, that we can shrink, by our striving, that gulf between the us we are and the us we ought to be and, just maybe, one day get across.

When John the Baptist is continually questioned about his standing with regard to Jesus in John 3, he finally says that Jesus "must increase, but I must decrease" (v. 30). In other words, we should increase our need for Christ, rather than work to decrease it. Our resolutions should look less like a register of achievable goals and more like the demands of the Sermon on the Mount: a terrifying list of requirements that force us to our knees. We should know, looking at that gulf between our real and ideal selves, that, should we attempt to jump it, we would surely be dashed to pieces on the rocks below. This year, resolve to turn the other cheek. Every time. Resolve to love your enemies. Even the ones who hurt you. This year, resolve to never have a lustful or an angry thought. If those are your resolutions, you'll end this year having cried out for the saving grace and mercy of Jesus Christ more than you did last year.

We attempt to tell ourselves that a happy year is one in which we get closer to the other side of that divide between the us we are and the us we ought to be, if not finally reach that far shore. A truly happy year, though, is one in which we come face to face with our need for a savior and hear the Good News proclaimed: our savior has come, laid down his perfect divinity for our benefit, and died on our behalf. Our savior Jesus Christ's work is complete, and that's why God has given him "the name that is above every name, so that at the name of Jesus every knee should bow, in heaven and on earth and under the earth, and every tongue confess that Jesus Christ is Lord" (Philippians 2:9-11).

Our savior has come and he has done his work, and brought us, as the Book of Common Prayer puts it, "out of error into truth, out of sin into righteousness, and out of death into life."

Those of us in Christ do not merely celebrate a new year. We celebrate a new life.

A RICH YOUNG MAN

What must I do to be saved? This is a question that we ask ourselves with regularity. Thankfully, we have a good answer, as it is a question asked directly of Jesus. That answer, though, is not what we might expect. In Mark 10:17-27, far from talking about faith in God or dependence on him, Jesus talks to his questioner about his money. The rich young man who wants to know how to be saved says he's been keeping the commandments (do not murder, commit adultery, steal, bear false witness, or defraud...and honor your father and your mother) since his youth. He's basically telling Jesus that those things are easy! Child's play!

So Jesus says, "You lack one thing: go, sell all that you have and give to the poor, and you will have treasure in heaven; and come, follow me." Mark says that the man was shocked to hear this "and went away sorrowful, for he had great possessions."

As we continue to consider the move from difficult to impossible that Jesus and the Bible encourage, this story—and the concept of stewardship—will provide a helpful illustration. Many churches, perhaps yours included, use the "tithe," or 10% of income, as the standard of "good" stewardship. But that number doesn't seem to come into Jesus' thinking. After all, a tithe is a difficult requirement. As we've seen, though, Jesus isn't interested in difficult. He's interested in impossible.

Notice that Jesus doesn't ask this rich young man for 10%... for 25%...or even 50%. He asks him for everything! Apparently, for Jesus, the standard for "good" stewardship is nothing less than donating every single thing you own and keeping nothing for yourself. You can't claim to be a good steward until you've given everything away to follow Christ.

Faced with a standard like this, it's no wonder that the disciples whispered to each other, "Then who can be saved?" Who can be good enough? Who can be a good steward? Jesus' response to their fearful question is one of the most comforting sentences in all of Scripture: "With man it is impossible, but not with God. For all things are possible with God."

As you consider your stewardship of not only your money but of all of your Christian life, remember that the same principle holds true of all Christian spiritual discipline: it's not about maintaining your good standing with God. If it was, the only acceptable offering would be 100%! I don't know about you, but I'm going to come up short of that standard. I'm just kidding by the way; I *do* know about you: it is impossible for us to be good stewards!

That's why we can think of stewardship—and, indeed, the rest of the Christian life—a little bit differently. We're not trying to be good stewards. The standard is too high. So with the pressure to be good removed, we can think about what we are actually moved to give. Think about what you actually want to do. Just know, as you consider your giving of yourself, as you think about living out your Christian life in your community, that your relationship with God is secured forever by the gift of Jesus Christ, not in the size of any gifts that you might give or in the quality of any ministry you might do. God, in Christ, has accomplished the impossible: he has made you a good steward, and he has made you a good and faithful servant.

CHOOSE THIS DAY

At the beginning of the criminally underrated Luc Besson film *The Fifth Element*, an alien species is retrieving a weapon that they stashed on earth in the run-up to World War I. Trust me:

it's awesome. As the retrieval is happening, things start going wrong—because of Luke Perry (again, awesome)—and it looks like one of the aliens is going to die. Everything is crumbling around them, a wall is literally closing in on them, and a human priest, who is helping them, shouts to the alien, "There's no time!" And the alien, with his final breath, says these powerful words: "Time not important. Only life important."

Only life is important. So: what is life? I actually think that most of us would probably agree on a general definition of life, and I think we'd find our ideas backed up by what Moses tells the people of Israel:

> See, I have set before you today life and good, death and evil. If you obey the commandments of the LORD your God that I command you today, by loving the LORD your God, by walking in his ways, and by keeping his commandments and his statutes and his rules, then you shall live and multiply...But if your heart turns away, and you will not hear,...I declare to you today, that you shall surely perish.... Therefore choose life, that you and your offspring may live... (Deuteronomy 30:15-19).

Pretty simple, right? Life is a choice—or a long series of choices—and if you make the right ones, you will prosper; make the wrong ones, and you will suffer—"I have set before you today life and good, death and evil."

This makes total sense to our human intuitions, right? Cause and effect, actions and consequences. Do you turn left or right? Red pill or blue pill? Who among us isn't subconsciously living this way? "If I just make all the right decisions—the right choices—things will turn out okay. If I can just keep things on the right path, everything will be fine." We're all driving the cars of our lives with white knuckles, desperate to keep them between the white lines.

This, my friends, is no way to live your life. In fact, I'll submit to you that this isn't life at all. It's death. Does that sound like an overstatement? I don't think it is. This "life" that we live, where happiness, health, and peace of mind hinge on every decision that we make actually makes happiness, health, and peace of mind impossible. It's a brutal death-march marked by stress, anger, and failure. Examine your life! I suspect you already feel this way. I do.

We make the wrong decisions *all the time*. Nothing turns out quite the way we want it to, and our percentage is so bad that even when things are going *well* we're still waiting for the other shoe to drop. So what happens? We become paralyzed, terrified to make *any* decisions lest we get another shock or something else in our lives goes wrong. This is death. It's a living death…a walking death…we're still upright and breathing, but make no mistake: we're dead.

So what went wrong? It seemed so simple! We set out to avoid the bad things and to choose the good! What happened? How did we end up here?

In Joshua 24, right before his death, Joshua gathers the people of Israel together at Shechem (much like Moses is doing outside the promised land in Deuteronomy), and he says these famous words:

> Now therefore fear the Lord and serve him in sincerity and in faithfulness. Put away the gods that your fathers served beyond the River and in Egypt, and serve the LORD. And if it is evil in your eyes to serve the LORD, choose this day whom you will serve, whether the gods your fathers served in the region beyond the River, or the gods of the Amorites in whose land you dwell. But as for me and my house, we will serve the LORD. (14-15)

And the people say, "We would *never* serve anyone but God!"

This is the first decision in their life's decision tree—which god to serve—and they're certainly not going to get the first thing wrong! *Of course* they're going to serve the God of Abraham, Isaac, and Jacob. But then Joshua says something fascinating. He says, "You are not able to serve the LORD, for he is a holy God."

Moses, similarly in Deuteronomy, puts the choice to the people—choose life or death—but he doesn't (because he can't) give them the *ability* to follow through on their choice. Joshua delivers the bad news: the commandments have a weakness. They may tell you what to do, but they cannot give you the ability to do it.

The choice seems obvious for us, too: obey the commandments, choose life, do the right thing, worship God. And all the people say, "Amen! We *will* do those things." But as we know so well, in our actual lives, we don't. We turn left instead of right, we take the blue pill instead of the red pill, we don't do the things we want to do and we do the things we don't want to do, and all of a sudden, everything is going to hell and it's all we can do to put ourselves together a little bit so that the disaster that's going on inside doesn't show through too much on the outside. Thus, the truth is revealed: we don't have the ability to do the things we set our minds to. We are disabled. Remember Junior Seau? We wake up each morning and recommit to choosing what is good, right, holy, and beautiful... and we go to bed each night begging for forgiveness for how we lived the day. This is why we need a better answer than the law, something more helpful than a rulebook. Moses cannot have the final word.

Praise God, he doesn't. Here's the Good News: When Moses said "Choose life," Jesus Christ said, "I am the life." Moses in Deuteronomy 30:19: "I have set before you life and death, blessing and curse. Therefore choose life, that you and your offspring may live." Jesus in John 14:6: "I am the way, and the truth, and the life. No one comes to the Father except through me." In other words, no one, by their own choosing, gets to God. We get to God by Christ. The law says that we have to make the right choice to inherit life. The Gospel says that Jesus Christ is life, and that *he* has chosen *us*.

As Christians, we believe this to be the truth. It's written right into our worship. When we baptize, we don't baptize into "Gosh, I hope they make the right choices…" because, as we've seen, that wouldn't be baptizing them into life! A child who is given the burden of making good choices is being baptized into walking death! We actually do baptize into a death, but we baptize into *Christ's* death.

A life lived under the pressure of "choose wisely" is no life at all, but is actually a living death. In Christ, the *us* that had to choose wisely has been put to death, once and for all. We have been created anew: we are no longer the ones who choose, but the ones who are chosen. My friend Jonathan Linebaugh put it this way: "Being dead is *having* to live. Being alive is having died. Trying to live by your own strength is death. Dying in Christ is being raised to new life."

There is Good News: life and death are no longer up to you. The you that had to choose, did choose, and died. Now a savior has come, one who gives new life to the dead, who is Christ Jesus. He is the life, and he chooses to give his life to you.

WHILE WE WERE SLEEPING

In Genesis 15, God makes Abram—the patriarch who has not yet become Abraham—a promise. But Abram is skeptical. God has already told Abram that from him he will make a great nation, that his descendants will be more numerous that the stars in the sky. This, we read, Abram believes. But then God said to him, "I am the LORD who brought you from Ur of the Chaldeans, to give you this land to possess." Now Abram has a doubt. He says to God, "O Lord GOD, how am I to know that I shall possess it?"

Abram might as well be saying, "Great promise God! How do I know that it's true?" Sound familiar? We hear the amazing promises of God, who allegedly so loved the world that he gave his only Son, that whoever believes in him should not perish but have eternal life...and we wonder, "Can it be true? How can we know for sure?"

So God sets out to show us. He knows our doubt, so he decides to prove his faithfulness. He knows his promises sound unbelievable, so he turns us into believers. Now, the way he decides to show Abram his assurance—with a bunch of animals sliced in half—seems very strange to us, but was in fact very commonplace back then. When two parties entered into a covenant, this ceremony is how they ratified it. They would get a bunch of animals, cut them in half, and lay them out, making a path between them. Just like the last time you closed on a house, right? Then, each party entering into the covenant would walk between the divided animals, in effect saying, "If I violate this covenant—if I break my word—may I end up like these animals." You can think of it as an ancient version of "cross my heart and hope to die, stick a needle in my eye," which, when you think about it, is just about as grisly as anything we've got going on in Genesis. This is the ultimate "I promise." The parties entering into this covenant are staking their very lives on their faithfulness to it.

And that's what makes this covenant between God and Abram so incredible, and such a moving illustration of God's grace. When it comes time to ratify the covenant, God puts Abram to sleep and passes—symbolized by a smoking fire pot and flaming torch—between the animals alone. Take a moment to let the implications of that soak in. Do you see what this means? By passing between the animals alone, God is saying one thing we expect, and one thing we can barely comprehend: He says, "If I break my word to you, it's on me." Sure. That makes sense. That doesn't surprise anybody...that's how these covenants are supposed to work! But he also says something earth-shattering: "Even if you break your word to me, if you're the violator...it's still on me." God promises to uphold *both sides of the deal.* In this world of "you give me mine and I'll give you yours," our God is talking about a one-way love. From him to you. His love, given to you. His faithfulness, given to you. His righteousness, given to you. Abram's relationship with God doesn't depend on Abram at all! In fact, Abram is so uninvolved in this deal that he not only doesn't pass between the divided animals, God puts him to sleep for the whole ceremony! This is the illustration we've been given to help us understand our covenant—our relationship—to God. There is no illustration more passive than this: an uninvolved—no, an unconscious!—human being receiving the benefits of a promise from an active God. He is good. We are asleep. And when we awaken, the deal is done, and we are saved.

The other night, I told one of my kids that as a consequence for some bad behavior, he wasn't allowed to read books at bedtime. He was understandably sad, but I didn't truly understand the depth of his sadness until I assured him that he could read books the *next* night. "You don't know that," he said. "Well sure," I responded, "as long as you're a good listener!" And that's when the true sadness came, along with a true confession: "Maybe I won't be. What if I'm not?"

Maybe I won't be. What if I'm not. Sound familiar? Great promise God! How do I know that it's true? And that's when it hit me: We don't actually doubt that God's not good enough to keep his promises, we doubt that we're good enough to deserve them. When we hear his promises, that he sent his Son to die for us, that he will be with us to the end of the age, that he loves us, and we say, "Great promise, God! How do I know that it's true?" we're not afraid that God is going to welch on his promises. We're afraid that he'll look at us and say, "This promise is too wonderful for the likes of you."

Isn't that the fear beneath all our fears? That God's promise is too wonderful for the likes of us? But that's what this ceremony with Abram is all about! The promise is too wonderful for the likes of us...but it doesn't depend on us. You're not good enough to deserve what God has given you, but God doesn't give his gifts on account of you. He gives them on account of Christ! We did, in fact, fail to uphold our end of this covenant, but God did, in fact, on the cross, take the weight of our failure onto himself. This is the very essence of the Gospel. When we are faithless, he is faithful. The Third Day song I mentioned in the last chapter, "Take My Life," has additional lyrics that speak to God's inexhaustible faithfulness:

> How many times have I turned away?
> The number is the same as the sand on the shore,
> But every time you've taken me back.
> And now I pray you do it once more.
> How many times have I turned away?
> The number is the same as the stars in the sky,
> But every time you've taken me back.
> And now I pray you do it tonight.

Every time. And here's the proof: our God's love is not conditional. He holds up both ends of the bargain. When we don't deserve his love, he calls us his sons and daughters, not on account of anything we've done, but on account of Christ. While we were sleeping, he saved us.

CHAPTER 10

YOUR IMPOSSIBLE SAVIOR IS CHRIST

The astute reader will no doubt have noticed that there are no stories about Jesus mentioned in the chapter on the impossible in Scripture. Like a comedian withholding the punchline, I was saving them. The stories featuring Jesus, the ones where God accomplishes the impossible, are the proverbial punchline to the good news inherent in the act of admitting that your life is impossible, rather than difficult. When our lives are impossible, we stop trying to save ourselves and allow Jesus to be our savior. Even in the several stories in this chapter that don't feature Jesus, the rescues are so profound as to point directly to Jesus' accomplishment on the cross.

Remember that Derek Webb song I keep coming back to? "A New Law"? The one with the line, "What's the use in trading a law you can never keep for one you can that cannot get you anything?" As we saw in Chapters 7 and 8, when we lower God's standards and requirements from impossible to difficult, it becomes possible to think that we can function as our own saviors. After all, if Ethan Hunt always completes his mission—proving it to be difficult rather than impossible—why can't we? But as Webb so beautifully notes, in God's economy, adherence to a lower standard doesn't get you anything. Jesus says so himself when he cautions his listeners:

> "Whoever relaxes one of the least of these com-
> mandments and teaches others to do the same will
> be called least in the kingdom of heaven, but who-
> ever does them and teaches them will be called great
> in the kingdom of heaven. For I tell you, unless your
> righteousness exceeds that of the scribes and Phar-
> isees, you will never enter the kingdom of heaven."
> (Matthew 5:19-20)

It's only the law you can never keep that could—if only you could keep it—get you something. Thankfully, the Gospel is the Good News about Jesus Christ, the one who came not to save the proficient, but the failure. He didn't come to reward those who are successfully clearing the high jump bar. He came for those who knock it down at embarrassingly low heights (Luke 5:31-32). God's first work is to show you how high the bar is, to show you that your life is impossible. God's final work is to send his only son into the world to clear that bar for you.

THE INNER AND OUTER CHRIST

Barry Zito, winner of the 2002 Cy Young award, was then the best pitcher in baseball. It wasn't to last long. Just a few years later, in 2006, after signing a huge free agent deal with the San Francisco Giants, he became…well, not the best. Due to his huge contract, he became one of the most derided players in the sport, considered someone who never lived up to the $126 mil-lion he was paid. As evidence, note that when the Giants made the playoffs in 2010, they left Zito off the roster completely and went ahead and won the World Series without him.

Then, a few years later, something fascinating happened. During the 2012 playoffs (and eventual World Series victory), Zito began pitching better, against all expectations. In a subsequent *ESPN The Magazine* interview, he took a stab at explaining why. His grandmother, he revealed, had, in the 1960s, founded a religion and teaching center called "Teachings of the Inner Christ," and Zito had been raised in its cocoon. It wasn't until 2011 that Zito says he committed his life to God.[5] He admitted to relying on his own strength for all those years and finally realizing that he had "to go through difficulty and physical trials to really get broken down." When his eyes were opened to his damaging self-reliance, his phrase is powerful: "Man," he says in the interview, "I'd been wearing it." You can hear the exhaustion. Finally able to shrug off that burdensome yoke, he realized that he needed to find a strength outside himself. "The way I was raised," he admitted, "that's a concept I never would have given any credence." Zito went on to share a powerful illustration:

> I had this very odd injury in April of 2011...and I came off the field that day after never being hurt in 11 years, and I said, "All right, something bigger is going on here. A message is being sent, and I've got to listen." ... My best friend told me an old story I really love. A shepherd will be leading his sheep, and one of the sheep will be walking astray from the pack. The shepherd will take his rod and break the sheep's leg, and the sheep will have to rely on the shepherd to get better. But once that leg is completely healed, that sheep never leaves the side of the shepherd ever again. That's a really beautiful metaphor. A lot of things happen to us as people, and we realize we've been relying on our own strength for too long.

Doesn't the name of Zito's grandmother's religion just say it all? "Teachings of the Inner Christ," indeed. This is a perfect illustration of the difference between a difficult life and an impossible one. As long as life is merely difficult, an Inner Christ—a self savior—might be all you need. But not when things get really bad. Not when things get impossible. Zito found that he needed a savior from without (let's call him the Outer Christ—Jesus of Nazareth), since the one from within wasn't doing him any good. The illustration Zito chooses is instructive too, as it can only be seen as a good thing from the perspective of a healed sheep. In the moment? To the sheep which has just had its leg broken? God might not seem such a sympathetic figure. As Tullian Tchividjian says in his book *Glorious Ruin: How Suffering Sets You Free*, "God doesn't save you from suffering, he saves you in suffering." The potentially disturbing metaphor of a shepherd breaking the leg of a sheep takes on a much more compassionate tone when you understand that shepherd himself has suffered and died for the lives of each one of his sheep.

Barry Zito needed more than the bondage of an "Inner Christ." Only the freedom that came from a reliance on the Outer Christ—the real Christ, Jesus—allowed him to pitch well. He never suggests that this is a path recommended for others, or that it will necessarily produce "results." Results become, if anything, a natural outgrowth. Note how much of all of this is natural, rather than chosen. It took a "very odd" injury for him to have his eyes opened. Our eyes are opened in an odd way too. We would never choose to have our legs broken by the shepherd…which is why God must come from without to open our eyes to the depths of our need, and to the glorious truth that there is a good shepherd there to nurse us.

FIVE THOUSAND MOUTHS TO FEED (LUKE 9:10-17)

It's one of Jesus' most famous miracles: a hungry crowd, a young boy, five loaves and two fish, and twelve baskets of leftovers. As a newly ordained minister, I was surprised to discover that the story of Jesus' miraculous provision for an enormous crowd was one of the first sermons to stop me in my tracks. Though it seems like a great, straight-forward story, as I thought about it, I discovered that the feeding of the five thousand is actually a hard story to preach. It's like the many healing stories in the Bible: all well and good for the people who got healed, but what about everyone else in the crowd? Perhaps more to the point, what about everyone out there in the pews who's not getting healed? What about them? Sure, Jesus can feed five thousand with five loaves and two fish, but what's he doing about the thousands of homeless people who show up to churches and missions every day? They might get a meal today, but what about tomorrow? Oh, and what about you? It's great to hear this story about needs being so radically met, but what about your needs? It's all well and good that Jesus can make such a miracle happen, but where's your miracle? Where's my miracle? I was once talking about this parable with another preacher, and he said to me, "People want God to meet their needs in the same radical way. But I know I'm going to be preaching to many people whose needs aren't being met. And that's where I get stuck." There is good news: Jesus is the God of the stuck. Listen:

> And taking the five loaves and the two fish, he looked up to heaven and said a blessing over them. Then he broke the loaves and gave them to the disciples to set before the crowd. And they all ate and were satisfied. And what was left over was picked up, twelve baskets of broken pieces. (Luke 9:16-17)

The thing that always gets me about this story is Jesus' looking up to heaven and giving thanks. Maybe that's a no-brainer to you; after all, many people probably say some form of thank-you to God before every meal! But would you think to say grace when you're sitting around a table that doesn't have enough food on it? Jesus has so much confidence—unlike me—in God's ability to provide that he thanks God even though he doesn't have enough! Now, we might say a prayer before sitting down to such a meal, but it wouldn't be a prayer of thanks, would it? I'd say a prayer for more food! But at least we're getting God involved, right? See, Jesus understands a profound truth: when you're presented with an impossible situation (five loaves and two fish for 5,000 people), you're going to have to get God involved. We can all look at the situation that Jesus found himself in—too many people, not enough food—and admit that, without God, it's impossible. Better call on the big guy, then, we say. And look what happens! Five loaves and two fish feed 5,000 with no problem, and there are twelve baskets of leftovers. That's our powerful God at work, finding a way to make the impossible possible, and everything's great.

Only God makes the impossible possible. For you to have a good relationship with your stepchildren, God has to get involved. For brothers and sisters to reconcile, God has to get involved. To be in a healthy relationship with your coworkers, God has to get involved. To love—truly love—another person, God has to get involved. For the impossible to become possible, God has to get involved. And when God gets involved, the impossible is accomplished. Sadly, due to the brokenness of the world, the unhealed, the homeless, and the poor will always be with us. The final redemption of the world, however, has been completed in Christ.

WAITING FOR LAZARUS

Perhaps the most famous Biblical example of Jesus as Impossible Savior is in the story of the death and subsequent resurrection of Jesus' friend Lazarus. Word comes to Jesus that Lazarus is very sick. Though the Bible is explicit that Jesus loves Lazarus, as well as his sisters Mary and Martha, Jesus stays two more days "in the place where he was" before going to answer the call to the dying man's bedside (John 11:5-6). Jesus is waiting for the difficult (healing a sick man) to turn into the impossible (raising a man from the dead).

When Jesus gets to Lazarus's tomb, he instructs the gathered people to open it. They're worried, though, because Lazarus has, at this point, been dead for four days and will very likely have begun to smell. These four days have another significance. Due to the relatively primitive nature of medicine at the time, people would occasionally revive even after being pronounced dead. So, three days was the generally accepted time frame for a person to be really and actually dead. Lazarus hadn't made a peep in four days. He was really and actually dead.

We human beings are all too often like Martha, who says to Jesus (when he first arrives on the scene, before Lazarus is raised), "Lord, if you had been here, my brother would not have died" (John 11:32). This is what I'm getting at: we want a Jesus who heals the sick because we don't trust him to raise the dead. Mary and Martha thought that as long as they could get Jesus involved before things got too out of hand, everything would be okay. If Lazarus died, though, it would be too late.

Remember the scene in *Avatar*, when an attempt is made to save Sigourney Weaver's life by literally plugging her into Eywa, the movie's version of a nature goddess? Eywa is powerful, and can heal, but Sigourney Weaver is too far gone. She has died and there's nothing Eywa can do. Eywa is a goddess of the difficult, but not the impossible. Mistakenly, we think of Jesus in these terms all too often.

It comforts us to think of our relationship to Jesus as though we're a home he's thinking of buying. We know we're not perfect, and so we think of ourselves as a "unique fixer-upper opportunity." You know, there's some termite damage behind the drywall, the kitchen could use some updated appliances, and maybe another coat of paint or two in a couple of the bedrooms. Nothing too serious. In fact, this could be our refrain to Jesus: "Nothing too serious!" We sing this refrain for two reasons.

First of all, we don't think of Jesus as being able to do the more serious work. He can do the touch-ups, improving the wonderful people that we already are. Our refrain of "nothing too serious" goes well with the hypothetical song "God helps those who help themselves." We'll take care of our foundations, thank you very much, not that they need much work. And that really leads us into the second, and much more common, reason: We don't really think much work is necessary. We don't think that our situation is that dire. When St. Paul writes about the human condition in Romans 3, we don't think that there's any way in the world that it could apply to us:

> What shall we conclude then? Do we have any advantage? Not at all! For we have already made the charge that Jews and Gentiles alike are all under the power of sin. As it is written: "There is no one righteous, not even one; there is no one who understands; there is no one who seeks God. All have turned away, they have together become worthless; there is no one who does good, not even one." "Their throats are open graves; their tongues practice deceit." "The poison of vipers is on their lips." "Their mouths are full of cursing and bitterness." "Their feet are swift to shed blood; ruin and misery mark their ways, and the way of peace they do not know." "There is no fear of God before their eyes." ...for all have sinned and fall short of the glory of God... (3:9-18, 23, NIV)

This hurts. It's devastating to be told that your beautiful house is so terribly beset by structural problems that it's going to have to be torn down and rebuilt. We just want a little contact with

Jesus; we think that he'll take the good stuff that we've got going on and capitalize on it. We're not perfect, we'll admit that... but foundationally? We must at least be okay there, right?

Jesus' answer is simply, "No." He only does complete gut jobs. He refuses to do anything less than tear things down to the foundation and build something completely new. He said that anyone who wanted to be his disciple needed to take up his cross and follow him (Mark 8:34). Carrying crosses isn't so common now, but when people did carry crosses? Back in Jesus' day? There was only one way that walk ended. You didn't put the cross down, you ended up on it. Jesus is saying that to be his disciple, you've got to die. And we, who think we're only sick, who think that God helps those who help themselves, we say, "Whoa whoa whoa! I only came for a little help!" Like Monty Python's Black Knight, we insist that it's just a flesh wound. "I'm a unique fixer-upper opportunity," we protest, "not a total gut job! Nothing too serious!"

Jesus, though, has got something serious in mind. Jesus has the stone rolled away and commands Lazarus to come out. Lazarus comes out, and Jesus is proved once again to be able to accomplish the impossible. When Martha came to Jesus, he said, "I am the resurrection and the life. Whoever believes in me, though he die, yet shall he live, and everyone who lives and believes in me shall never die." If we're honest with ourselves, Paul's description of us is dead on: ruin and misery mark our ways. We're more than sick. We're falling apart. But Jesus Christ is a God who does something so much better than heal the sick. He raises the dead to new life.

A WALK TO REMEMBER

I was a pretty good baseball player as a little kid (though I never sniffed the Little League World Series), and I loved it, too. Every spring, I would unwrap the rubber band from around my glove and put it on the brim of my new hat; everything was just right. And I was one of the funny ones: I looked forward to practice, even more than games. Because you see, my favorite part of the sport was fielding, and in a game, you might get a couple of balls hit to you a day. During infield practice, though, the coach would just hit you grounders over and over again. It was heaven. I had one coach—when I was probably 11 or 12—who was this grizzled stereotypical guy, all the expensive gear and the large beer gut, a guy who had played in college thirty years ago and who wasn't going to take it easy on us little kids because the world wasn't going to take it easy on us, you know? I remember he would hit grounders at us as hard as he could. And on those small little league fields it could get pretty crazy. On more than one occasion, a ball would take a funny bounce and crack a kid's nose, bust a lip, or bury itself in your you-know-where. You'd be writhing around, trying to recover from the last ball, and the next one would be screaming toward you, accompanied by a yelled "encouragement," like, "Come on, son! Rub dirt on it and keep going!" "You think those other teams are gonna take it easy on you?" "I could come field grounders for you, but what good would that do?" or "Figure it out or I'll find somebody who will!" It was sink or swim. You had to be able to face down a ball hit harder than any that any kid would probably hit at you. Then, the grounders you'd get in a game would seem easy. My plan was always to throw myself into these grounders face first. If I didn't field them cleanly, I could at least impress the coach with my hustle.

The story that Matthew tells (14:22-33) of a stormy sea, of Jesus (successfully) and Peter (briefly) walking on water, is the Biblical analog to this. Or at least, it appears to be so at first blush. Jesus is the grizzled coach. Peter is the exuberant rookie. He's the kid with the hustle. He says, "Lord, if it is you, command me to come to you on the water." Can you imagine?

The faith of Peter is rightly lauded! He's got the guts to step out of the boat, onto the water, and start walking. Peter was a fisherman! He's got lots of water experience! He must know what happens to people who are in the water but not in a boat. They sink! But—for just a moment—he doesn't. Peter is actually walking on the water. But then what happens? Matthew says that he notices the strong wind and becomes frightened. That, then, is Peter's critical mistake. He was faithful enough to begin his walk on the water...but not faithful enough to finish it. He took his eyes off of Jesus. Don't make that mistake!

I once ran across a children's sermon outline which suggested that the preacher tell the gathered children to look at him, and to not to take their eyes off of him, no matter what happens. Then, you were supposed to tell the kids to focus on you as your prearranged adult volunteers try to distract them, turning the lights turn on and off, spraying kids in the face with water bottles, and playing a storm soundtrack over the speakers. Then you ask, "Was it difficult to keep your focus where it was supposed to be? Just imagine Peter's distractions: the wind was howling and the waves were crashing. Peter turned his focus to the things around him and he doubted Jesus. He was gripped with fear and he began to sink."

Then, the application section of the outline has you say that Peter had a mixture of faith and fear. He started out with faith, but finished in fear. It included a line that I'll never forget: "You know the kind of fear I'm talking about—the kind that makes you feel like there's a whirlwind in the pit of your stomach." And then the teaching point: stay focused on Jesus.

And listen, this is all fine. It's actually pretty good advice. After all, we should stay focused on Jesus. We shouldn't let our fear convince us that God doesn't have sufficient power or that he doesn't care. And I love the way this fear is described: "the kind of fear that makes you feel like there's a whirlwind in the pit of your stomach." Who can't identify with that? The only problem with the admonition to stay focused on Jesus is that it assumes we're not already sinking! But we are. Wherever you're reading this: you're drowning. You need so much more than pretty good advice.

If I encourage you to have the faith of Peter, to believe in the power of Christ so strongly that you're willing to get out of that boat and walk on the water, but then I admonish you not to make the mistake that Peter did—don't take your eyes off of Jesus!—I'm assuming that you're either still in the boat or still successfully walking on the water. "Get out of that boat! Have powerful faith!" I might be saying. Or, "You can do it! Keep walking on that water! Finish the way you started! Keep your eyes fixed straight ahead on Jesus!" The problem is, if you're anything like me, or my family members, or any of my friends, you know—maybe only subconsciously—that exhortation and admonition come too late. You don't need good advice. Or encouragement to step out in faith. Or admonishment to do better. Your problems aren't difficult. They're impossible. Your marriage fell apart. Your worst secret just became public knowledge. A child has stopped talking to you, or a parent has failed you completely. You're drowning.

There is Good News for drowning people. And the Good News is this: Christianity is not ultimately about good advice, exhortation, or admonition. All those things have their place, and used in their place can be a great benefit. But they are not good news for drowning people. This is: "But when [Peter] saw the wind, he was afraid, and beginning to sink he cried out, 'Lord, save me.' Jesus immediately reached out his hand and took hold of him."

Jesus doesn't wait. He doesn't say to himself, "Let's see how Peter reacts. Will he be able to extricate himself from this difficult situation?" Jesus doesn't hit Peter another ground ball as hard as he can. Matthew says that Jesus' reaction is immediate. He reaches out his hand to save.

This story is not about staying focused on Jesus, although that's a good thing. It's about *knowing that Jesus is focused on you*. Jesus is not a tough love coach who's not gonna do it for you, not gonna take it easy, and really wants you to figure it out for yourself. In fact, Jesus would be a terrible coach because, instead of asking for an accomplishment from you and encouraging you to do your best, he gives you his own accomplishments! He actually does step in and do it for you! At first, he's much worse than my little league coach: he doesn't just want effort and hustle. He asks not just for hard work but for perfect obedience: "Love your enemies. Give all you have to the poor. Be perfect, as your heavenly Father is perfect." But then, after being worse, he becomes so much better: after asking for perfection, *he gives his perfection as a gift*. He takes all your failure onto his shoulders and gives you all his goodness in exchange. Christianity is not about a Jesus who stands there encouraging us to swim more efficiently. Christianity is about a Jesus who rescues the drowning.

Now, I can hear your objection: "I bet you guys got really good at baseball with that demanding coach!" And yes, the law, exhortation, encouragement and admonishment can lead to temporary obedience. But here's the thing: *it never leads to love.* We hated playing for that coach, and I can't even remember his name. People who see Jesus as a tough love coach? A coach who wants them to accomplish the difficult? They give it a shot for a while, get burned out, and then leave forever...and they run so far away that they don't even remember his name. People who know Jesus as the savior who rescues the drowning? A savior from the impossible? They fall in love with him forever.

So when you feel that fear—and you know the fear I'm talking about, the one that makes you feel like there's a whirlwind in the pit of your stomach—don't delude yourself. Don't think, "What can I do to stay on top of the water?" or "What does my coach want me to do?" Do what Peter did. Say, "Lord, save me!"

The Buddha's final words were "strive unceasingly." Sounds like my old coach, doesn't it? Jesus' last words were, "It is finished." I'll take Jesus, thank you very much, because it's too late for me to strive. I'm drowning. I'll call out with Peter, "Lord save me."

JESUS' JOB DESCRIPTION

Matthew 5—as we've seen throughout this book—contains some of the hardest verses in the entire Bible. In his Sermon on the Mount, Jesus cautions us that whoever "does...and teaches" the commandments—even the smallest ones—will be called great in the kingdom of heaven. That sounds fine, until he goes on to say that our righteousness must exceed that of the scribes and Pharisees, or we will never enter that kingdom. He goes on to say that anger (and thinking someone a fool) is morally equivalent to murder, that lust is morally equivalent to adultery, and—in the final indignity—that his requirement is that we be perfect, even as our heavenly Father is perfect (Matthew 5:48).

Most Christians know these verses very well. We also know the verses that kick off Matthew 5—known as the Beatitudes—very well: "Blessed are the poor in spirit, for theirs is the kingdom of heaven. Blessed are those who mourn, for they shall be comforted. Blessed are the meek, for they shall inherit the earth..." and so on (Matthew 5:3-11).

It's astonishing to me, though, how easily we read over the verses that come *between* the Beatitudes and Jesus' radical redefinition of the law's requirements. Ask anyone what they remember about the Sermon on the Mount, and chances are they'll talk about the Beatitudes and about the law...but listen to the verses that come between those two sections: "Do not think that I have come to abolish the Law or the Prophets; I have not come to abolish them but to fulfill them. For truly, I say to you, until heaven and earth pass away, not an iota, not a dot, will pass from the Law until all is accomplished" (Matthew 5:17-18).

Do you hear what Jesus is doing here? Yes, he's giving an incredibly difficult job: You think the law says don't murder? I say the law says don't be angry. You think the law says don't commit adultery? I say the law says don't lust. You think the law says do your best? I say that you must be absolutely perfect. *But he's not giving this difficult job to us.* This is Jesus assuring his people that he has come to fulfill the law! This is Jesus' job description, not yours!

Jesus' mission in the Sermon on the Mount is to make sure that no one can look at his mission and think that it's difficult. He makes it impossible. Don't be angry. Don't lust. Be perfect. With a job description like that, we don't need a miracle once in a blue moon...we need a miracle every day. We need a miracle right now. And this is the miracle we have: Jesus taking this job description onto himself, promising to fulfill the law, accomplishing the impossible for us.

GOD COMES TO HIS ENEMIES...US

One of the most counter-intuitive passages in the Bible—and one of the most comforting—comes in the fifth chapter of Romans. Paul is talking about who God comes to, who he pursues, who he wants to be in a relationship with. Here's what he says:

> For while we were still weak, at the right time Christ died for the ungodly. For one will scarcely die for a

righteous person—though perhaps for a good person one would dare even to die—but God shows his love for us in that while we were still sinners, Christ died for us. Since, therefore, we have now been justified by his blood, much more shall we be saved by him from the wrath of God. For if while we were enemies we were reconciled to God by the death of his Son, much more, now that we are reconciled, shall we be saved by his life. (Romans 5:6-10)

So God acts in this wildly unexpected way: he doesn't come looking for the good people, he comes looking for the bad. He doesn't come looking for the strong, he comes looking for the weak. He doesn't come looking for allies…he comes looking for enemies.

One of the central tenets of Christianity is the doctrine of the incarnation. That refers to God becoming one of us, a human. And while this might seem like sort of a no-brainer, sort of a snooze, for us—since we've heard the Christmas nativity story for our entire lives—the idea of almighty God becoming one of us was originally considered to be one of the most unbelievable things about our faith. It was seen as impossible.

In the history of human religion, there was and has always been this idea that God is pure, holy, and most importantly, separate from humanity, in order to preserve his purity and holiness. When the first Christians started saying that Jesus was God "incarnate," many people rejected it out of hand, not because of anything specific about Jesus—that he didn't look right, or act properly, or say the things that he was supposed to say—but because they assumed that God *by definition* wouldn't defile himself by coming to a dirty place like Earth and occupying a dirty thing like a human body.

The Christian claim that God has come to be one of us sets it apart; makes it unique. Every other religion sets up a paradigm in which the worshipper has to purify him- or herself, either by acts of devotion, self-denial, good works, or hours of meditation. Through work—self-purification—the worshipper has to get to God. Only Christianity offers a God that comes to you. Only Christianity has a God who doesn't wait for you to get to him. The Christian God, in Christ, crosses the chasm—from clean to dirty—to get to you.

THE GOD WHO DOES EVERYTHING

The God of Christianity is counter-intuitive, sometimes in the extreme. He just doesn't work the way that we expect him to. Those "normal" ways that we think God works (that we discussed in Chapter 3) get turned on their head by a God who doesn't wait for you to get to him but who comes to you first. He doesn't help those who help themselves. He helps those who cannot help themselves. He doesn't wait for you to go one yard before he goes ninety-nine. He gives his victory to you before you've even come out of the locker room. He's not a gentleman, waiting for you to open the door on which he's patiently knocking. He doesn't need a handle on his side of the door. He's kicking it down. He is a doctor, come to rescue the sick. He's come not for the righteous, but sinners. He's in the resurrection business. He is capable of accomplishing an impossible mission.

Recall the image of the Christian life: a fence around a mountain. The vast majority of people—even Christians—imagine that Christ came to open the gate in the fence. He gives us access, but now it's up to us to climb. Jesus gets us in, but we have to keep ourselves in. Jesus "gets us right with God," but now we've got to "live out the Gospel." That phrase, by the way, is a nonsensical one; the Gospel cannot be "lived out." It is news, an announcement that Jesus came into the world to save sinners.

A God who does everything, though, destroys the normal way we think about the fence and the mountain. A God who does everything—who, remember, passed between the animal carcasses by himself—simply picks you up from outside the fence and places you on top of the mountain. Jesus has achieved the summit, and has given that accomplishment to you.

A God who does everything does so much more than wipe your slate clean. Because of the work of Jesus on the cross, your slate is not just clean, but filled edge to edge with Christ's successes. This, perhaps, is the most impossible thing of all. All your failures, erased and replaced. All your faithlessness, erased and replaced. His life for yours. His righteousness for your sin. His goodness for your badness. It just doesn't seem possible. But in Christ, the impossible is accomplished.

GOD'S WORKSHOP

One of the logical results of God doing the impossible must be that he is always at work where we least expect it. We've seen that throughout this book. We expect him to assist his children, to give them the push they need, to help them cross the finish line. But that's not what he does. The difficult is not where he is at work. Instead, the impossible is God's workshop. It's where he makes miracles. He delights in accomplishing the impossible, most personally in the redemption of a sinner like you (and me). There is perhaps no clearer illustration of this principle than Jesus' interaction with (so-called) "Doubting" Thomas.

Remember when you would mercilessly make fun of some uncool kid in school because you were deathly afraid of people realizing how uncool you yourself were? I don't know, maybe you were confident in your coolness...all I can say is that I was always on the lookout for the kid who was even less cool than me, because believe you me, I was going to make sure everybody else noticed, too. That's probably what was going on with whoever started calling Thomas—who, you'll note, used to be called the Twin (see John 20:24), a much cooler nickname—"Doubting" Thomas. I can imagine the disciples getting together and saying something like, "We've been messing up royally for weeks straight…but let's start calling Thomas 'Doubting' Thomas…maybe people will cut us some slack!" And it worked. We've been calling him Doubting Thomas ever since. But maybe we shouldn't be.

You know the story well (John 20:24-29): Thomas isn't with the disciples when Jesus comes back the first time, and he doesn't believe them when they tell him that Jesus is risen. Then Jesus shows up, offers Thomas his wounds as proof of the resurrection, and tells Thomas not to doubt, but to believe.

When we picture that scene, of the risen Christ appearing to Thomas—Doubting Thomas—and when we reflect on the many scenes of Holy Week, we almost can't help but think, "Gosh, I'd like to think that I wouldn't have made all of those mistakes." Or at the very least, we decide that we're going to buckle down and become the kind of people who don't make those mistakes *from now on*. But both of those attitudes—that we'd never make the mistakes the disciples did or that we're going to commit all our energy to not making them in the future—are actually us running away from the fundamental, painful, and embarrassing truth of our lives: that we are the people who make those mistakes. We are just like Jesus' idiot disciples. We are the people who think that it's inappropriate for Jesus to be a servant, washing our feet. We are the people who, when the chips are down, claim—both by those things that we do and those things that we do not do—that we do not know that man from Nazareth. We are the people who can't wait upon Jesus for even one hour…especially not if something better comes up. We are the people who shout for Barabbas, the revolutionary that we really wanted Jesus to be. We are the people, by our every subconscious attempt to justify ourselves without Jesus' help, who shout, "Crucify him! Crucify him! We don't need him!" We are the people who, even having heard all of Jesus' teaching, might well have approached the tomb on Easter morning thinking that we'd find his body there. And finally, we are the people who doubt everything, unless we see it with our eyes and touch it with our hands. We are just like the disciples. We are Doubting Thomas.

There is Good News for us. Jesus comes to Thomas! Thomas doubts, and Jesus comes. There has never been better news! And even when it looks like it's about to turn into bad news, when it appears that Jesus is giving Thomas a command—"Do not doubt, but believe," seeming to put the weight of responsibility back onto Thomas's shoulders—it's only after he has come to Thomas, offering the wounds in his hands and in his side. Taken properly, this is not so much Jesus commanding Thomas to believe, but something more like a name-changing ceremony, celebrating a new faith.

Remember, this is what Jesus does! This is his *modus operandi!* He comes into a situation with an undeserving person and he redeems it, and them. He makes something new. In this case, he gives Thomas a new nickname. That's what "Do not doubt, but believe" is really all about. He's not giving Thomas a new job, he's giving Thomas a new name, the best nickname of all time. "You're not Doubting Thomas anymore," he says. "Now, you're Believing Thomas. Faithful Thomas."

And he does the same for you and me. I'm Doubting Nick. You're Doubting Mary, or Doubting Sam, or Doubting William, or Doubting Jessica. Doubting You. But Jesus comes to the doubters. He comes to the faithless. He comes to you and me, holding out his marred, wounded hands, and he gives us each new names. When once we were called sinful, faith-less, and doubting, he calls us his beloved brothers and sisters. He calls us righteous. He calls us faithful. I'm Faithful Nick. You're Faithful Mary, or Faithful Sam, or Faithful William, or Faithful Jessica. Faithful You. By his work on the cross and his resurrected life, he gives us the faith we lack, accomplishing the impossible by turning a doubter into a disciple. His work enables us to echo Faithful Thomas: "My Lord and my God."

The impossible is demanded everywhere in Scripture—from stem to stern and from Genesis to Revelation. But every time God demands the impossible, he provides a way out, a rescuer, a Savior.

So what now?

CHAPTER 11

CHRISTIANS GROW IN REVERSE

Perhaps you've heard the phrase, "The more you know, the more you know you don't know." The idea is a simple one: as you get smarter, you become more and more aware of how much more knowledge there is out there. In other words, the smarter you get, the more you realize how low on the total knowledge ladder you are. The same can be said of Christianity. The more mature in Christ you become, the more aware you are of your immaturity.

Mother Teresa—years after her death—became a poster child for this idea when her own spiritual doubts and feelings of separation from God became public knowledge. This woman who had seemed to be such a paragon of faithfulness had, in fact, written in a letter to a friend that "Jesus has a very special love for you. As for me—the silence and the emptiness is so great—that I look and do not see—listen and do not hear." These words were written mere months before Teresa received the 1979 Nobel Peace Prize, and shed light on a profound truth: the most mature Christians are not those whose moral character permits them to rely on Jesus less; no, mature Christians are those who are so closely attuned to their sinfulness that they know exactly how much they need him. Christian growth, then, is not a progression upward, from weakness to strength. True Christian growth is more properly to be thought of as a progression downward, from assumed strength to acknowledged weakness. As we grow as Christians, more and more things do not become possible for us. In fact, we grow more and more aware of just how impossible everything is outside of Christ.

HERO TO ZERO

Han Solo has a classic movie character arc. At the beginning of *Star Wars*, he's in it only for himself, right? He shoots Greedo to get out of paying a debt—and yes, Han shot first—and he agrees to take Luke and Obi-Wan to Alderaan…for the right price. And even after they end up on the Death Star, he only agrees to help rescue Leia because he's promised wealth beyond his imagining. He doesn't care at all about the rebellion. But at the end of the movie, after seeming to leave like a selfish coward, he zips into the fight, saving Luke and saving the day. It's a classic story. And the movies love stories like this, because we all love stories like this. The rascal who learns to have a heart of gold: this is the kind of story arc we like best. We all want to be Han Solo. It's a redemptive arc, an improvement arc, a triumphant arc. From bad to good. From zero to hero.

Speaking of "zero to hero," have you seen the incredible film *Cool as Ice*? Can you guess that it stars early 90s rap icon Vanilla Ice? Anyway, in the film, Vanilla Ice plays a really cool guy—I know, you're shocked—and you can tell he's cool because his hair is super slicked and he's got notches shaved into his eyebrows. He falls in love with a girl who already has a boyfriend. But since he's Vanilla Ice starring in a movie called *Cool as Ice* and he's got notches shaved into his eyebrows, he doesn't let the fact that she's already got a boyfriend stop him. In fact, he has a suggestion, and he utters these immortal words: "Baby, you gotta drop that zero and get with the hero." This is the direction we like, the Han Solo arc. From zero to hero. It's the way we're all trying to go.

In Matthew 16, though, we have a character who seems to be moving in the other direction. If most movie heroes go with Vanilla Ice, from zero to hero, the Apostle Peter seems to be going from hero to zero!

Beginning in verse 13, we read the story of Jesus and his disciples in the villages around Caesarea Philippi: "He asked his disciples, 'Who do people say that the Son of Man is?' And they said, 'Some say John the Baptist, others say Elijah, and others Jeremiah or one of the prophets.' He said to them, 'But who do you say that I am?' Simon Peter replied, 'You are the Christ, the Son of the living God.'"

When Jesus asks the disciples about his identity, it is Peter who is the hero. He's got the right answer! "You are the Christ." And then Jesus tells Peter that he is the rock upon which his church will be built. Now we know, theologically speaking, that Peter is not actually the rock upon which the church is founded. The church is founded on Peter's confession of Christ as the Messiah, not on Peter himself. But the illustration still stands. Peter gets the answer right and he's rewarded! A gold star! This isn't the first time, nor will it be that last, that Peter is the hero. When Jesus comes walking on the water, it is Peter who gets out of the boat and stands on the water himself. When Jesus says at the last supper that one of the disciples will betray him, it's Peter who says, "No way, Lord, not me. Even if I have to die, I won't betray you." These are heroic things to say. So it doesn't seem strange that Jesus verbally rewards Peter for his confession, even changing his name from Simon to Peter, which means "rock."

In fact, it's during this name changing ceremony that everything seems to go south for Peter. Scripture says that "from that time" (Peter's correct confession of Jesus) "Jesus began to show his disciples that he must go to Jerusalem and suffer many things from the elders and chief priests and scribes, and be killed, and on the third day be raised."

And Peter, who was just the hero, who must have felt like he was sort of on a roll, tries to stay a hero, and begins to rebuke Jesus. He makes his heroic stand: "Never, Lord!" he said. "This shall never happen to you! I'll never let anyone kill you!" But to Jesus, in this moment, Peter goes from hero to zero. Jesus turns and says to Peter, "Get behind me, Satan! You are a hindrance to me. For you are not setting your mind on the things of God, but on the things of man."

This is how fast Peter's transition from hero to zero happens. In a paragraph! In one breath, he gets the answer right ("You are the Christ, the son of the living God") and becomes the hero. But then, in the next breath, when Jesus starts to talk about what's going to happen to him, Peter tries to be the hero by claiming that he'll prevent Jesus' death, but goes to zero real fast: "Get behind me, Satan!...For you are not setting your mind on the things of God, but on the things of man."

Okay, so in the space of five sentences, the amount of time it takes Vanilla Ice to shave those cool notches into his eyebrows, Peter goes from the rock upon which Jesus is going to build his church, to the embodiment of Satan himself. And how does Jesus explain himself? What is Jesus' teaching in the face of this huge slide? This fall from hero to zero? What does he have to say to Peter? What advice does Jesus have for his followers? "If anyone would come after me," Jesus says, "let him deny himself and take up his cross and follow me. For whoever would save his life will lose it, but whoever loses his life for my sake will find it."

Peter's mistake is in trying to save Jesus' life! His mistake is trying to be the hero! We make this same mistake, too. We try, every day, to live lives that are good. Lives that would make Jesus proud. We know we're not perfect, but I believe that we think that if we do well enough, maybe Jesus won't have to die for us. We'd like, like Peter, to keep Jesus off that cross if we can. Of course, it happened in the past, so our only recourse is to try to become people who wouldn't have needed something so intense, thank you very much. Now, I know you'll say, "No! I don't think that! I'm glad Jesus died for me!" And, of course, we are! I'm with you! But stop. Take a second. Wouldn't you rather? Wouldn't it be nice if the son of God hadn't had to die for you? Wouldn't it alleviate some of the pressure if you could say, "Well, I'm one less person he had to suffer for," or "He didn't have to suffer quite so much for me," or "Unlike me, *that* guy really needs Jesus." Have you ever caught yourself having a thought like that? Every day, we try to do the honorable thing, the heroic thing: we try to save Jesus' life. We're like people shouting at the screen in a scary movie: "Don't go in there!" We say, "Don't pick Judas to be a disciple!" At his trial: "Defend yourself!" Carrying the cross: "Don't walk up that hill!" Finally, we say, "You have the power! Command the angels! Come down from that cross! Please!" We're with Peter! We want to save Jesus' life! And, to that attitude, Jesus says, "Get behind me, Satan!...For you are not setting your mind on the things of God, but on the things of man."

Jesus' disciples thought that being his followers meant protecting him, keeping him safe, saving his life. But Jesus, in some of his most profound words, says that it's only people who carry crosses who can follow him, and that the way to salvation is through death. Make no mistake: followers of Jesus go to the cross with him. Hear me clearly: I'm not saying that followers of Jesus *need* to go to the cross with him. I'm saying that followers of Jesus are actually on their way to the cross. It's not a commandment, it's happening. If we try to save him, if we avoid the cross, we lose ourselves. All too often, we think "carrying our cross" means a sort of picking-ourselves-up-by-the-bootstraps, walking a hard road, soldiering on with a thorn in our flesh, making the best out of a hard life...not giving into temptation. We say things like, "Well, that's just my cross to bear." We forget too easily that people who carry crosses end up on them, 100% of the time. But that's the amazing thing! When Jesus asks us to take up our crosses and follow him, our figurative deaths are traded for his physical death. Jesus' cross stands in for ours. Our separation from God was traded for his closeness with God. Our sin was traded for his righteousness. Jesus said, "Take up your cross and follow me," knowing full well that not one of his disciples could bear the weight. Peter, the rock, denied his best friend, the one he called "the Christ, the Son of the living God," denied even knowing him, three times, only a few hours after saying he'd die for him. We're with Peter, on the precipitous slide from hero to zero. We want to save Jesus' life. We say, like Peter did, "Jesus, I'll die for you." But we've got the direction wrong! We are the zeros, he is the hero. We must decrease, and Christ must increase. When we cry out, "Jesus, I'll die for you!" Jesus, knowing our sin, our weakness, our pain, and our fear, says, "No," and he dies for us instead.

SPELUNKING

I became a more mature Christian in the parking lot of my dentist's office, when I locked my keys in my car. Perhaps you're thinking now that that's not the kind of situation that would inspire you toward Christian maturity...but let me tell you why. I realized that I locked the keys in the car on the way *into* the dentist, so I had to sit there as they scraped away at my teeth, trying to figure out what to do about it. Luckily, we have roadside assistance coverage through our insurance, so I was able to call and get someone dispatched to help me. It was actually pretty slick: they used my cell phone to triangulate my exact location, and the service generated an automatic text with an ETA only about thirty minutes away. Everything was going to be fine. But then, the ETA came and went, two phone calls to the roadside assistance provider came and went, and three phone calls to the actual guy in the truck came and went. Finally, it's two and a half hours later, I'm going to miss picking up my kids from school, and I'm frothing at the mouth. The guy can't find me, even though I'm in the parking lot of a business and they allegedly used my cell phone to triangulate my exact position! The names I called that driver, the roadside assistance company, and my insurance company, down in the deepest recesses of my heart, were nothing short of despicable. It was a level of hate that surprised me. When the guy finally came to let me into my car, I said as few words to him as possible, worried about what might come out if I let my mouth stay open too long. Finally, with my harrowing ordeal behind me, I got the kids, got home, and waited impatiently for my wife to get there so that I could tell her how I'd had to deal with such inconsiderate idiots all day.

Impressive, right? Can't you just feel my new maturity when you read that story? But I'm actually not being sarcastic. I honestly do think I grew as a Christian because of that experience. Let me explain...and I've got a great illustration to help me:

> "Two men went up into the temple to pray, one a Pharisee and the other a tax collector. The Pharisee, standing by himself, prayed thus: 'God, I thank you that I am not like other men, extortioners, unjust, adulterers, or even like this tax collector. I fast twice a week; I give tithes of all that I get.' But the tax collector, standing far off, would not even lift up his

> eyes to heaven, but beat his breast, saying, 'God, be
> merciful to me, a sinner!' I tell you, this man went
> down to his house justified, rather than the other.
> For everyone who exalts himself will be humbled,
> but the one who humbles himself will be exalted."
> (Luke 18:10-14)

Now, you've probably heard this story a dozen times, and you've heard stories that make this point a thousand times. You probably didn't even get a couple sentences into the above quote before you skipped to the end. "We get it, all right?" I can hear it now: "The Pharisee is a self-righteous jerk and the tax collector has a healthy awareness of his sin and of his need for a savior. Don't be the Pharisee, be like the tax collector." But take a moment. Look closer. Is the Pharisee a self-righteous jerk? What does he actually say? "God, I thank you that I am not like other people: thieves, rogues, adulterers, or even like this tax collector. I fast twice a week; I give a tenth of all my income." He's not actually a self-righteous jerk, he just thinks he's a mature spiritual person! He even thanks God for his spiritual maturity, and doesn't seem to take much credit for himself. He sees the good gifts that God has given him, sees how far he's come, and he says thank you. Surely that's not so bad, is it?

The problem is that the Pharisee has spiritual maturity completely backward. In the Pharisee's conception of spiritual maturity, and most other people's, too, the path of Christian growth is like the path up Mt. Kilimanjaro. It's a long, hard walk, but anyone who sets their mind to it, trains properly, and has the right equipment can do it. Maybe we Christians don't need to lift weights, eat properly, or get the right hiking boots, but we have the equivalent, don't we? We need to spend some devotional time with God, perhaps in prayer or fasting, we need to read God's word in Scripture, and we need to give of our financial resources to aid the ministry of the church. A mature Christian sounds a lot like that Pharisee, doesn't it? But we're not going to make the same mistake this Pharisee made, are we? No, we're too smart for that! Remember, don't be like the Pharisee.

But do you see what we've just done? We just put ourselves two pews over from the Pharisee! He's looking over at and judging the tax collector, so he doesn't see us looking over at and judging him! "God, I thank you that I am not like other people: fundamentalists, my mother-in-law, or even this Pharisee. I keep my ever-growing spiritual maturity to myself."

This, then, cannot be what spiritual maturity or Christian growth is about. And in truth, Christian growth isn't like climbing Mt. Kilimanjaro. It's more like a spelunking expedition descending into Mammoth Cave, shining a light into all the nooks and crannies that are full of spiders, gross worms with no eyes, and horrifying insects. Jesus enters the caverns of our hearts and shines his light into all the corners of sin that we didn't even want to acknowledge to ourselves: the lust, the pride, the everything that we hide away from everyone. We say, "No! Stay out!" "Yes," he says, "I have come to redeem even that." Spiritual maturity isn't about getting better and better and seeing fewer and fewer people around you in the pews who can measure up to the standard you're setting; no, real spiritual maturity is about the light of Christ shining into ever deeper and darker unexplored corners of your sinful heart. Christian growth comes from being reminded, once again, in a dentist's office parking lot, just how much and how desperately you need Jesus.

The true shape of Christian growth is captured perfectly by Robert Lowry's classic hymn "I Need Thee Every Hour." He writes:

> I need Thee every hour, most gracious Lord,
> No tender voice like Thine can peace afford.

I need Thee every hour, stay Thou nearby.

Temptations lose their power When Thou art nigh.

I need Thee every hour in joy or pain.

Come quickly and abide or life is in vain.

I need Thee, oh, I need Thee, every hour I need Thee.

Growth in Christ—advancing spiritual maturity—means an ever-growing acknowledgment of how much we need Jesus. Every hour. Every moment.

But even this is not the real climax of the story. It's all well and good for the tax collector (and for us) to acknowledge our crippling need, to refuse even to look up to heaven. But that can't be the end! "We're not worthy!" is not good news! We can't stop there. And praise God, we never stop there. We worship a God whose property is always to have mercy on the unworthy.

This is why the tax collector goes home justified. Not because he's so adept at beating himself up, but because of God's answer to his tortured cry.

He says, "Be merciful to me, a sinner!" and God—in Christ—says, "I will have mercy on you." For us, the news is even better because it's already accomplished! God says, "I have sent my son to live for sinners like you, to die for sinners like you, and to be raised again for sinners like you."

There are two ways in which your sin can surprise you. First, like me in the dentist's parking lot, you can be surprised at the darkness of it, the anger that you're capable of, and the fact that your heart is more twisted that you ever thought it was. Or, you can be surprised to find yourself in the Pharisee's pew, looking around and thinking, "Thank goodness I'm not like these terrible sinners. Is there a way to differentiate between them and me?" Either way, the realization will wring a tortured cry from your throat: "Oh my God, I had no idea…be merciful to me, a sinner. I need Thee every hour, most gracious Lord."

God, the Father of our savior Jesus Christ, answers our cry: "I am your peace. I am nearby. My Son has died for you. I have given you my pure heart in exchange for your twisted one. I have given you my goodness in exchange for your sin. You need me. I am here. I always will be. Every hour. Every moment. Always."

CHAPTER 12 √3/23/20

LIFE IS IMPOSSIBLE...AND THAT'S GOOD NEWS

Every day, we wake up faced with an impossible mission. Unlike Ethan Hunt and the IMF, our mission is *actually* impossible, and we will fail. Honor your father and mother. Be a good parent to your child. Be a good provider for your family. Don't commit adultery, and remember that anyone who looks at someone with lust in their heart is an adulterer already. Don't commit murder, and remember that anyone who has a moment of anger toward anyone is a murderer already. Turn the other cheek when your enemies attack you. Love the people who don't love you back. And the hits just keep on coming.

God routinely demands the impossible from us. This is the story of the Bible, and the story of our lives. But then, incredibly, he provides the way forward. Remember those five loaves and two fish. They weren't enough. Full stop. Neither are we. But Jesus looks up to heaven, thanks God, and makes a way. Our God loves to do the impossible. Bringing an enslaved nation out of Egypt? Difficult. Our God brings them through the Red Sea. The impossible, made possible. Healing a sick person? Difficult. Our God waits until Lazarus has been dead for four days to bring him back to life. The impossible, made possible.

Our God has given us a holy standard to live up to that we each fail to reach. We fail every single day. But Jesus succeeds every single day. Every single day a miracle happens: Jesus gives his success to us.

PREDICTING THE WEATHER

At the end of the underrated Gore Verbinski film *The Weather Man*, Nicolas Cage (who plays the titular weather man) has come through an incredibly difficult period in his life. He's spent a lot of time and energy trying (and failing) to impress his father. He's spent a lot of time and energy trying (and failing) to win back his estranged wife. He thinks that by getting the big national weather man job, he can do both of those things. By the end of the film, he's accomplished all the things that he thought would get his life back on track...and his life isn't back on track. His final words of the film are, "Come on. Another man's with my family. Things didn't work out the way I predicted. Accepting that's not easy. But easy doesn't enter into grown-up life."

He thought achieving his dream life would be difficult: he had to get the dream job. But it turns out that even getting the dream job doesn't accomplish what he hoped it would. His dream life turns out to be impossible to reach. But, counterintuitively, this realization doesn't crush Cage. In fact, it was the effort in the face of the difficult that was crushing him. The realization that his life is impossible actually gives him peace.

After a film full of Cage claiming—when he's approached on the street—that he's not the weather man people keep thinking they recognize from TV, he's recognized one final time. After signing an autograph, the fan looks up at the sky and says, "So, is it going to rain today?" With a wry grin, Cage says, "Who knows?" This is brilliant. Cage is able to acknowledge his powerlessness—after all, who can accurately predict the weather? Who is in control of their life?—and have peace in the face of it. Once the impossible has been acknowledged, its power over him withers away. The same is true for you: acknowledge the impossible and your powerlessness, and its power over you— completely and utterly outshone by the power of your savior— fades away completely.

In Christ, God accomplishes the impossible once again: a sinful person saved. Your mission impossible was laid on Jesus' shoulders. Every time you don't turn the other cheek, Jesus did. Every time you hate, Jesus loved. Every time you sin, Jesus carried it to the cross. Every time you tried to climb the invisible ladder of success to get to God, God sent Jesus Christ down to get to you. Every single time. So today, and every day, as you consider the failures of your life, the goals you set for yourself, and the person that God asks you to be, remember that Jesus' words on the cross weren't a whispered "Earn this." They were a shouted "It is finished!" It is in light of that finished work of Christ—the impossible accomplished—that we celebrate: the impossible miracles of Jesus' life, given to you and to me.

ENDNOTES

1. A handful of short passages in this book draw inspiration from entries originally written by the author in *It Is Finished: 365 Days of Good News* by Tullian Tchividjian with Nick Lannon.

2. Hitchens, Christopher, and Jacques del Conte. "The New Commandments." *The Hive, Vanity Fair*, April 2010.

3. Burkeman, Oliver. "Who Goes to Work to Have Fun?" *The New York Times*, 11 Dec. 2013.

4. Robertson, Dale. "Bode Miller Wins Gold Medal in Super Combined." *Houston Chronicle*, 22 Feb 2010.

5. Browne, Rembert. "Rembert Explains America: Burning Man Forever." *Grantland*, 10 Sept. 2013.

6. Keown, Tim. "A Man in the Game." *ESPN* Internet Ventures, 1 Dec. 2012.

ABOUT THE AUTHOR

Nick Lannon is a 2000 graduate of the University of Arizona and a 2007 graduate of Trinity Episcopal School for Ministry, having studied Communications and Religious Studies while at Arizona and Systematic Theology and Ethics at Trinity. An avid movie-watcher, NBA fan and all-around couch potato (when he's not playing sports himself), Nick is fascinated by the intersection of the Gospel and everyday life.

Ordained in 2007, Nick has pastored Episcopal churches in Jersey City (NJ), Denville (NJ), and Louisville (KY). He has served as Editor-in-chief and Director of Content, Research, and Writing at LIBERATE, the former resource ministry of Tullian Tchividjian, with whom he co-authored *It Is Finished: 365 Days of Good News*. Nick currently serves as pastor of Grace Anglican Church in Louisville, Kentucky.

Nick grew up in northern Virginia and lived there until going to Arizona in 1996, harboring naïve fantasies about playing on the basketball team. He currently lives in Louisville with his wife Aya and three children: Hazel, Patrick, and Charlie.

ABOUT MOCKINGBIRD

Founded in 2007, Mockingbird is an organization devoted to connecting the Christian faith with the realities of everyday life in fresh and down-to-earth ways. We do this primarily, but not exclusively, through our publications, conferences, and online resources. To find out more, visit us at mbird.com or e-mail us at info@mbird.com.

ALSO AVAILABLE FROM MOCKINGBIRD

The Youngest Day: The Four Seasons in the Light of Grace, by Robert Farrar Capon

An Easy Stroll Through a Short Gospel: Meditations on Mark, by Larry Parsley

Exit 36: A Fictional Chronicle, by Robert Farrar Capon

Bed and Board: Plain Talk About Marriage, by Robert Farrar Capon

Unmapped: The (Mostly) True Story of How Two Women Lost at Sea Found Their Way Home, by Charlotte Getz and Stephanie Phillips

The Very Persistent Pirate: A Children's Book, by CJ and Maddy Green

Never Satisfied Until Satisfied in Thee: Finding Grace in 'Hamilton', edited by Tim Peoples and Cort Gatliff

The Man Who Met God in a Bar: The Gospel According to Marvin, by Robert Farrar Capon

More Theology & Less Heavy Cream, by Robert Farrar Capon

Churchy: The Real Life Adventures of a Wife, Mom, and Priest, by Sarah Condon

Mockingbird at the Movies: an anthology of essays by various contributors

Law and Gospel: A Theology for Sinners (and Saints), by William McDavid, Ethan Richardson, and David Zahl

A Mess of Help: From the Crucified Soul of Rock N' Roll, by David Zahl

Eden and Afterward: A Mockingbird Guide to Genesis, by William McDavid

PZ's Panopticon: An Off-the-Wall Guide to World Religion, by Paul F. M. Zahl

The Mockingbird Devotional: Good News for Today (and Everyday)

Grace in Addiction: The Good News of Alcoholics Anonymous for Everybody, by John Z.

Made in the USA
San Bernardino, CA
01 September 2019